D0916526

Walking
South Yorkshire

Design and production by Vertebrate Publishing, Sheffield
www.v-publishing.co.uk

Walking
South Yorkshire

Written by **Rob Haslam**

Copyright © 2010 Vertebrate Graphics Ltd and Robert Haslam

First published in 2010 by Vertebrate Publishing.

Reprinted with minor amendments in 2016.

All rights reserved. No part of this work covered by the copyright hereon may be reproduced or used in any form or by any means – graphic, electronic, or mechanised, including photocopying, recording, taping, or information storage and retrieval systems – without the written permission of the publisher.

ISBN 978-1-906148-21-8

Front cover photo: AVTG.
Back cover photos: Rob Haslam and David Coefield.

Photography by Rob Haslam, unless otherwise credited.

 All maps reproduced by permission of Ordnance Survey on behalf of The Controller of Her Majesty's Stationery Office. © Crown Copyright. 100025218

 Design and production by Jane Beagley.
www.v-publishing.co.uk

 Printed and bound in Europe by Pulsio.

Every effort has been made to achieve accuracy of the information in this guidebook. The authors, publishers and copyright owners can take no responsibility for: loss or injury (including fatal) to persons; loss or damage to property or equipment; trespass, irresponsible behaviour or any other mishap that may be suffered as a result of following the route descriptions or advice offered in this guidebook. The inclusion of a track or path as part of a route, or otherwise recommended, in this guidebook does not guarantee that the track or path will remain a Right of Way. If conflict with landowners arises we advise that you act politely and leave by the shortest route available. If the matter needs to be taken further then please take it up with the relevant authority.

Contents

Acknowledgements

Signposting in Ecclesall Woods.

I would like to thank Chris Kelly for checking the Barnsley walks, and Fran and Fred Pickering the Rotherham walks. We were all volunteer route developers for the Sheffield *Get Walking Keep Walking* project, a Ramblers Association initiative whose primary aim was to improve the health of people living in deprived urban areas of the city through participation in community-based walking programmes.

Introduction

This is more than a book of country walks. It is a journey through history, an exploration of South Yorkshire's rich rural heritage.

The mining of ironstone and production of steel were originally woodland-based industries, dependent on the production of charcoal, the fuel that fired the first blast furnaces. Forests were maintained and coppiced to ensure a sustainable crop. Recently, thirty-six ancient woods were restored under a Heritage Lottery funded programme called *Fuelling a Revolution: the woods that founded the steel country*. These little known sanctuaries of preserved woodland, grassland, wetland and heath are now a haven for wildlife and flowers, and a delight to explore from spring to late autumn.

Some are hidden away in the unlikeliest of places, close to the centres of Sheffield, Rotherham and Barnsley. Though well-used by the local community, the wider walking fraternity is largely unaware of their presence and the outstanding natural beauty on their doorstep.

Utilising an unmapped network of well-maintained legal footpaths alongside rights of way, this book explores thirty-one restored woods, relics dating from the Iron Age to the Industrial Revolution and the county's most popular countryside visitor attractions, including the great houses and parks built upon the wealth of coal and iron.

Every walk is accessible from the transport interchanges in Sheffield, Meadowhall, Rotherham and Barnsley, and the proximity of the M1 and M18 motorways places them within easy reach by car. However well you think you know South Yorkshire, I guarantee you will discover something new and amazing as you work your way through this collection of memorable walks.

Robert Haslam
Sheffield, March 2010

What is Ancient Woodland?

Tree planting was uncommon before 1600, so to be deemed 'ancient' a wood must have been in existence for over 400 years. Written evidence exists, but biodiversity is the main guide to age. Plants like bluebell, wood anemone and yellow archangel are the main indicator species.

Unlike recent plantations, ancient woods tend to be irregular in shape and enclosed by banks, ditches or walls to keep out grazing animals. Wooded areas that were unsuitable for farming, like steep-sided valleys, are also likely to be ancient.

The names of the *Fuelling a Revolution* woods provide further clues: Canklow, Treeton, Herringthorpe, Wincobank and Wath were all ancient settlements. Prior Royd and Hail Mary Hill belonged to religious orders before the Dissolution. Carr, Hang, Lees and Woolley are Anglo Saxon words describing different woodland features. Others are named after landowners from before the 17th century.

Fuelling a Revolution interpretive panel

Types of Ancient Woodland

Centuries of management and the introduction of non-native species radically altered the wildwood that cloaked Britain after the Ice Age. The elements that remain are classified as follows:

Ancient semi-natural

Man-managed oak and birch wood where the ecosystem has remained intact through natural regeneration. Elder, holly, hazel, hawthorn, dog rose and blackthorn comprise the shrub layer. Grass and seasonal plants like bluebells and wild garlic are the natural ground flora, though open areas are readily colonised by bracken and bramble.

Ancient semi-natural oak and birch wood

Ancient replanted

By the early 19th century many coppices had been partially cleared and replanted with non-native trees. The establishment of beech, sweet chestnut, sycamore, ash, elm, maple and wild cherry alongside the original oak and birch changed the environment. The indicator plants remain, but the shrub layer is less dense. In the case of beech it is almost non-existent. Ancient replanted is by far the most common type of ancient woodland found today.

Wet woodland

Tiny remnants can be seen in some of the *Fuelling a Revolution* woods. A shrub layer of elder, hawthorn and hazel grows alongside willow and alder. The lush ground flora contains species typical of marshland, including rushes, lesser celandine and willowherb. Invasive species like Himalayan balsam have thrived in this habitat. Herbs, sedges and ferns inhabit damp areas in all three types of wood.

History of Woodland Management

Even before the Industrial Revolution, woods were maintained by coppicing – the continuous harvesting of the poles that sprout from the base of a stump after a tree has been felled. Rather than regrowing a single stem, a cut tree regenerates by producing multiple shoots called stools, which grow at an accelerated rate due to the root system already being in place. Depending upon the product required, maturity can be achieved in as little as five years. To ensure an even rotational cycle, coppices in the *Fuelling a Revolution* woods were divided into compartments, planted and harvested at different times to provide a

Open beech wood

Wet woodland

Coppice stool

continuous supply of wood. Given space and light, single-stemmed trees will grow straight and tall. These were known as standards, oak being the most common. By law, a coppiced wood had to contain at least twelve standards per acre, and was hence known as a 'coppice with standards'.

Whitecoal, a similar product to charcoal, was used to smelt lead, but the advent of coke in the 18th century all but eliminated the demand for coppiced products. The woods were managed for mature trees only, the stools 'singled' by allowing only the best stem to grow. Many coppices were cleared entirely during the 19th century and replaced with non-native trees to create the ancient replanted woods we see today.

The majority fell into neglect during the 20th century and nature conservation suffered. One by one they passed to the local authorities, and as housing began to encroach – in many cases right up to the boundaries – more people began using them for recreation, forging miles of unofficial paths. Litter, fly tipping and vehicular damage were undesirable but inevitable side effects of increased usage.

Restoration

Though maintenance began in the 1970s there was no major funding until *Fuelling a Revolution* began in 2000. After carrying out surveys and initiating management plans, the transformation from forlorn and neglected back to the semi-natural landscape of old began. Clearance and thinning opened the canopy to sunlight, allowing the dormant shrub layer and ground flora to rejuvenate. Leaving standing and fallen deadwood improved the habitat for fungi, invertebrates and the creatures that feed on them –

Fungi growing on dead wood

rodents, birds and bats. Habitats like grassland, heath and wetland were revitalised. Access was improved, footpaths upgraded, environmental artwork commissioned, and seats and information panels installed. Since completion in 2005 the respective councils have continued to actively manage the sites for the benefit of wildlife and people.

Archaeological and Historical Features

Four Scheduled Ancient Monuments are visited – Roman Ridge, which runs through Wath Wood, the Bronze Age settlement in Canklow Wood and the Iron Age forts on Wincobank Hill and in Scholes Coppice.

Bell pits from early coal mining and Q pits from whitecoal burning are found throughout the woods. The Trans Pennine Trail, encountered on many of the walks, utilizes railway lines and tracks dating from the Industrial Revolution.

Worsbrough Country Park is packed with historical remains, including a working 17th century corn mill, a water pumping engine house and an 18th century blast furnace. Elsecar Heritage Centre houses a Newcomen Beam Engine and a steam railway. Wentworth Castle, Bretton Hall, Cannon Hall and Wentworth Woodhouse were built on the wealth of coal and ironstone mining. Virtually every walk has something of historical interest as well as scenery.

Roman Ridge in Wath Wood

Trans Pennine Trail signpost

Newcomen Beam Engine

Improved Paths

Many of the footpaths – particularly in the *Fuelling a Revolution* woods and Country Parks – have been overlaid to counteract erosion, mud or encroaching vegetation. That doesn't mean miles of tarmac; far from it. The surfaces are walker friendly and dry, not hard or stony. To differentiate these from natural paths I refer to them as improved. Most walks combine the two. Remember that mud and the onset of a shower can be encountered at any time of year, so dress accordingly.

Transport

Twenty-seven walks start from off-road car parks; all but two free of charge.

Using a combination of bus, tram and train, it is possible to reach every walk from Sheffield, Rotherham, Meadowhall and Barnsley – Meadowhall being the integral link.

The recommended website for information is **www.travelsouthyorkshire.com** You can plan your route from place to place or by clicking on the timetable finder. Enter the service number given at the beginning of each walk, your time and date of travel followed by the appropriate route and you are given the timetable and map you require. Alternatively, the Traveline number is **01709 515151**. The South Yorkshire Day Tripper will probably be the most economical ticket if you are combining public transport. Check the website for options. Remember to double check if travelling on Sundays and Bank Holidays, when there are reduced services and often no services on particular routes.

The walks in each section can be reached by bus from the travel interchanges in the centre of town, some perhaps directly from where you live. One or two require a little extra walking to reach the start, but nothing excessive.

The yellow tram route from Meadowhall to Middlewood via the city centre is useful and it will also soon be possible to catch a tram direct from Sheffield to Rotherham. Trains serving the walks in this guide:

- Sheffield to Doncaster via Meadowhall, Rotherham and Swinton.
- Sheffield to Leeds via Meadowhall, Rotherham, Swinton and Bolton upon Dearne.
- Nottingham to Leeds via Sheffield, Meadowhall, Chapeltown, Elsecar, Wombwell and Barnsley.
- Sheffield to Huddersfield via Meadowhall, Chapeltown, Wombwell and Barnsley.
- Meadowhall to Lincoln via Sheffield, Darnall and Woodhouse.

Grid References

A six-figure Ordnance Survey grid reference for the start points is provided at the beginning of each walk. For the uninitiated, these are taken from the relevant Ordnance Survey map, the number and name of which is provided. Read from left to right along the top or bottom of the map for the first two numbers and imagine the distance between the blue lines divided into tenths to estimate the third. Repeat the process using the numbers ascending the sides of the map to pinpoint the grid reference. In the example shown, the red triangle indicating the now closed Youth Hostel at Langsett is at grid ref: 212005.

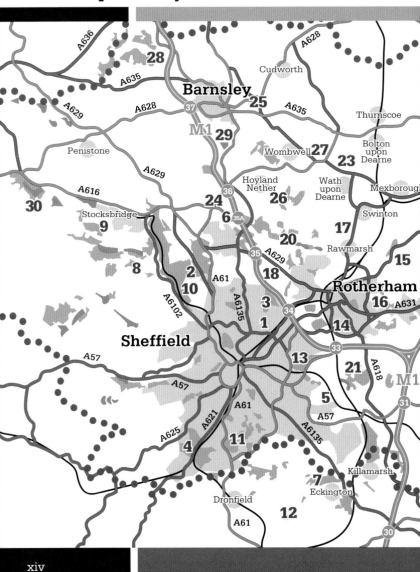

A key to the symbols used in the walks and on the maps:

 County borders

 Reservoirs and wetlands

 Woods, forests and green belt

 Railway line

 Refreshments

 Parking

 Accessible by bus

 Accessible by train

 Accessible by tram

 Accessible by car

 Start point

 Bus link

 Optional route

 Direction of walk

Sheffield

Sheffield claims to have more open space than any other city in Europe. 30% of the Peak District National Park lies within its boundary and, in all, 61% of the city is green space. Two thirds of the *Fuelling a Revolution* woods are located here and all 13 walks feature ancient woodland across the whole city, from the high moors of the Peak District through the rural fringes and into the suburbs. Combined with parks and local nature reserves, these semi-urban woodlands are a joy to walk.

Birley Edge.

Upper Moss Valley.

1 Wincobank Hill

Wincobank Hill is isolated from the surrounding urbanisation by its height. Its hog's back ridge boasts two scheduled ancient monuments, some open common, a Fuelling a Revolution wood and superb views of the city. We begin our walk from Sheffield's oldest park – Firth Park.

5 km / 3 miles

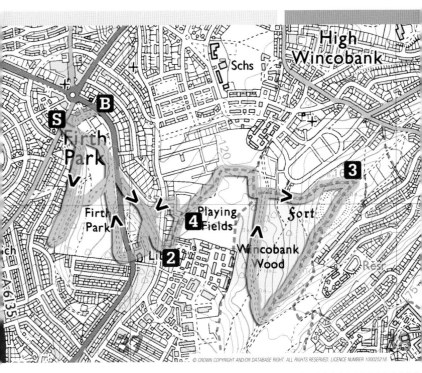

© CROWN COPYRIGHT AND/OR DATABASE RIGHT. ALL RIGHTS RESERVED. LICENCE NUMBER 100025218

START Firth Park car park on
Huculow Road.
GRID REF SK 368913.
PARKING Firth Park car park.
PUBLIC TRANSPORT
Bus services 1, 1a, 3, 75, 76, and 88.
Train from Barnsley and Rotherham
(or X78 bus) to Meadowhall, then the
3 or 35 to Firth Park.

TERRAIN Mostly improved paths,
with one prolonged ascent.
REFRESHMENTS Henry's Café in
Firth Park. Open every day
OS MAP Explorer 278, Sheffield,
Barnsley and Rotherham, South sheet.

1 Wincobank Hill

S Pass through the A-frame into the park, turn **right** at the signpost and **right** again on the narrower path downhill. 50m before the exit, double back **left** up steps through the wood. Climb a second set of steps into the park and continue down to Firth Park Road. Enter Hinde Common Wood just below the junction with Firth Park Avenue, branch **left** and follow the path through the centre of the wood. Pass two flights of steps and turn **left** up a few steps to the road.

The prominent hog's back ridge is surmounted by an Iron Age Hill Fort and is a panoramic viewpoint over much of South Yorkshire, a prime location for occupation in prehistoric times. The oval fortification is 2 acres in extent, surrounded by a single rampart and ditch. The thin acid heath supports heather.

2 Walk down Hindewood Close to the public footpath on the **left**, which leads to an area of common and an amazing transition. Keep to the improved path. Bear **right** at the fork and again into Wincobank Wood. Turn **left** on the stepped path to the summit of Wincobank Hill. Go **left** for 100m or so along the cobbled path for the view over Rotherham to the north-east and across the motorway to Keppel's Column before doubling back along the ridge.

During the late 19th century the Don Valley was producing 80% of Europe's steel. Imagine the catastrophic effect pollution must have had on this ancient wood. Illegal felling during the General Strike in the 1920s and the Second World War all but destroyed it. The wood was transformed through funded initiatives in the 1990s and Fuelling a Revolution.

3 As you begin to descend it is worth diverting a few metres at the opening on your left to stand on the ramparts and look out over the Don Valley. A little further down the city centre comes into view and then the Northern General Hospital appears to your right. To the left, across the flat area below the boulders, runs Roman Ridge, the second scheduled ancient monument on the hill. This 18km earthwork is seen close up on Walk 17. Turn sharp **right** and follow the improved path back through Wincobank Wood. Branch **left** beyond the wood and again to complete the circuit.

5 km / 3 miles

4   Instead of returning to Hindewood Close, bear **right** with the improved path to emerge higher up Hinde House Lane. Cross over into Firth Park Avenue and pass through the A-frame on your **left**. Descend the steps, turn **left** and then **right** down the next flight to the old lido. Turn **left** to re-enter the wood and pass to the rear of the Clock Tower. Turn **right** as you begin to ascend and then **right** to Firth Park Road. Cross and enter the park along a winding tarmac path. Follow this to the northern end or wander back across the grass to reach the First Start building, which houses a café and toilets.

The lido and Clock Tower, which housed a tea room and the park keeper's house, were the focal points of the original park, donated to the city in 1875 by industrialist Mark Firth and opened by the future King Edward VII. As the first in Sheffield it became enormously popular, attracting up to 30,000 visitors on Bank Holidays and 1,000 each day during the summer. It was expanded to include Hinde Common Wood in 1909. By the 1970s both park and wood had fallen into neglect. Regeneration began in 2000.

The Clock Tower, Firth Park.

2 Prior Royd & Birkin Royd

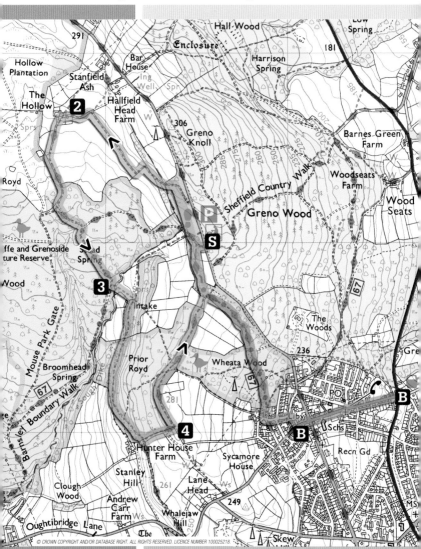

This is one of several figure-of-eight walks in this book. It can be added to Walk 10, *Wheata Wood & Birley Edge*, as they start from the same point, yet cover different areas. This shorter walk concentrates on two conjoined Fuelling a Revolution woods, with brief forays north and south into open country. The viewpoint at the southernmost point is widely regarded as one of the finest in Sheffield.

START Greno Wood car park on Woodhead Road, 800m north of Grenoside.
GRID REF SK 324951.
PARKING Greno Wood car park.
PUBLIC TRANSPORT
Bus service 85 to the Old Harrow Inn. Service 66 from Rotherham to Chapeltown then the 86.
Train from Barnsley to Chapeltown, then the 86. *The 86 stops on the main A61 by the Norfolk Arms. Walk up Norfolk Hill to the crossroads by the Old Harrow Inn and go straight on along Stephen Lane. Take the public footpath on the right after 100m. Turn left, pass an ancient water trough and at Middle Lane turn right on the TPT signed **Wortley**. Follow it to the car park, a distance of 2km.*
TERRAIN One steep climb. Stout footwear recommended.
REFRESHMENTS Pubs in Grenoside and on the A61.
OS MAP Explorer 278, Sheffield, Barnsley and Rotherham, South sheet.

2 Prior Royd & Birkin Royd

S From the car park follow the Trans Pennine Trail **right**, signed *Wortley*. At a fork by the second fingerpost branch **left** off the Trail to reach a corner of the wood. Descend with a wooded slope on your left and a field containing a telecommunications mast on your right. Pass through the gateway into the field and follow the edge around to the left. Halfway down turn **right** through the gateway alongside the hedge on your right.

2 Turn **left** to Hollows Farm and **left** again at the way-marker post along a muddy path with relief in places. Bear **left** and follow the wall into Wharncliffe Woods. Turn **left** at a T-junction, **right** at the next and descend to a fork. Leave the Trans Pennine Trail and cross the footbridge on your **left**.

3 Ascend the pasture to a signpost in the right-hand corner and turn **right** along the bottom of Birkin Royd. Turn **left** at a waymarker over a footbridge into Prior Royd. Join an improved bridleway and ascend. Where it swings sharply to the left, **continue straight ahead** on the upper path to a double stile. **Turn immediately left** and ascend alongside the wood to the summit and one of the best viewpoints in Sheffield; a massive sweep of countryside from the east, straight ahead, around to the south and the west.

4 Enter the wood and follow the Sheffield Country Walk over a path crossroads and along the easy-going trail. Pass through two wooden gates and bear **left** along the Trans Pennine Trail to the car park (or right to Grenoside for the bus).

3 **Woolley Wood & Concord Park**

Woolley Wood.

This pleasant walk begins along a branch of the Trans Pennine Trail, crosses Concord Park golf course and passes through a quiet area of Concord Park, leading eventually to one of the best Fuelling a Revolution woodlands in this book. Situated on the slope of a steep valley, Woolley Wood is particularly beautiful in late autumn, and in early May when the bluebells flower.

5.5 km / 3.5 miles

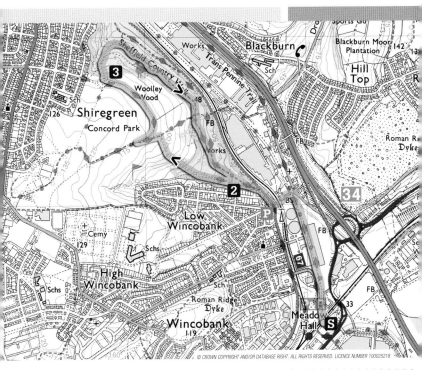

START Meadowhall Interchange for public transport, or Woolley Wood car park by the playground on the B6082, Ecclesfield Road, from where the route is 3.25km.

GRID REF SK 390913 (Meadowhall) / SK 387921 (car park).

PARKING Woolley Wood car park. (Meadowhall Park & Ride is free, but nearly always full.)

PUBLIC TRANSPORT Bus, tram or train to Meadowhall.

TERRAIN Improved paths throughout with one prolonged climb.

REFRESHMENTS Meadowhall Interchange.

OS MAP Explorer 278, Sheffield, Barnsley and Rotherham, South sheet.

3 Woolley Wood & Concord Park

Woolley Wood information panel

50m beyond the information panel you pass an intricate carving on a dead tree trunk, the first of three seen on this walk. They are the work of Jason Thomson, who did the Steel Giant, seen on walk 13.

As well as its stunning display of bluebells, Woolley Wood is noted for its preponderance of yew, hornbeam and huge wild cherry trees, all of which you will encounter on this walk.

S From the top floor of Meadowhall Interchange, cross the enclosed walkway to the car park and turn **right** down the steps. Join the Trans Pennine Trail, pass the Travelodge and continue along the Chapeltown branch of the Trail. Double back **left** before the next A-frame, cross Fife Street, turn **right** and **right** again at the traffic lights. Walk through the car park (**Alternative Start**) and ascend past the BMX track into the wood, passing a Woolley Wood information panel.

2 Keep to the wide main path, signed *Concord Park*, over a path junction by a golf tee and continue to climb. Emerge onto the golf course and cross the fairways to a junction with a Trans Pennine Trail signpost; turn **left**. Pass through an A-frame and turn **right** alongside the hedge. (You may prefer the grass to the tarmac through this secluded corner of Concord Park.) Continue through one A-frame alongside the hedge to another leading into Woolley Wood.

3 Follow the main path down steps into the wood and go **straight ahead** at a junction down more steps. Descend a good distance with a ravine on your left. At the point where a path branches left down yet more steps, continue **straight ahead**. The path undulates alongside a steep bank until it merges with a lower path by a seat and bends uphill past a wooden barrier. Turn **left** at a T-junction, 100m beyond which you will see the other two tree carvings and the runic Lost Gateway visible beyond. Turn **left** past the information panel back to the car park and to rejoin the outward route back to Meadhowhall Interchange.

Woolley Wood.

4 Ecclesall Wood

© CROWN COPYRIGHT AND/OR DATABASE RIGHT. ALL RIGHTS RESERVED. LICENCE NUMBER 100025218.

5.5 km / 3.5 miles

At 350 acres, Ecclesall Wood is the largest area of semi-natural ancient woodland in South Yorkshire. An oasis of beauty and calm, close to the city centre, it has been a popular local amenity for many years, in no small part due to the excellent signposting and footpath maintenance. No need, therefore, for it to be included in the Fuelling a Revolution programme.

START Ecclesall Woods Sawmill off Abbey Lane. The Woodland Discovery Centre is currently open 10am – 3pm Tuesday to Saturday.

GRID REF SK 322825 (Ecclesall Woods Sawmill) / SK 319835 (Ecclesall Road South).

PARKING Ecclesall Woods Sawmill or laybys close by on Abbey Lane.

PUBLIC TRANSPORT

Bus services Nearest bus is the 81, which stops outside the Toby Carvery on Ecclesall Road South. Turn onto Abbey Lane and into the woods to join the route at point **4**.

Train from Barnsley and Rotherham.

TERRAIN Mainly improved paths.

REFRESHMENTS The Rising Sun on Abbey Lane, 200m off the route. Open all day for real ale and food. *T* 0114 235 5071.

OS MAP Explorer 278, Sheffield, Barnsley and Rotherham, South sheet.

4 Ecclesall Wood

S Enter the wood through the gate beside the wooden shelter, cross the bridge and after 50m turn **left**. Cross a footbridge and turn **right** along the Abbeydale Road South bridleway. At the next junction, leave the wood through a gap and continue to a gate. Turn **right**, descend the steps and follow a stone-flagged path down to Limb Brook. Cross this, bear **left** and proceed along the Abbeydale Road South footpath to a T-junction.

Limb Brook is the main watercourse in a wood containing numerous small streams, all of which drain into the River Sheaf. Note this is an area of mixed woodland.

2 Turn **left**, cross a walled bridge and follow the riverbank to a gate. Leave the Sheffield Round Walk here and turn **left**. Cross Limb Brook and continue on the Abbey Lane bridleway. Go **straight ahead** at the next signed junction and bear **right** alongside the fenced bird sanctuary. Turn **right** at the bridleway to Abbey Lane.

3 Leave Wood 3 and cross the road into Wood 2, immediately branching **left** off the easy-going trail at the yellow arrow. Pass a path on the right and then a pond to reach the memorial headstone of charcoal burner George Yardley, who died in a cabin blaze on this site in 1786. Turn **right** at the junction, cross Whirlowdale Road and continue along the bridleway to Dobcroft Road, well signed throughout. Cross two streams in quick succession and turn **left** along the footpath to Abbey Lane.

4 Shortly before the path leaves the wood (bus stops) turn **left** on the footpath to Whirlowdale Road. (If seeking refreshment, the unsigned path going right at the next signed junction leads to Abbey Lane. The Rising Sun is to the right.) Cross the road, re-enter wood 3 and bear **left** at the junction for the sawmill.

PHOTO: Jon Barton

5 Shirtcliffe Wood from Flockton Park

A hidden gem, combining ancient woodland, parkland, field paths, good views and a sense of remoteness that belies its situation amongst Sheffield's eastern suburbs.

6.5 km / 4 miles

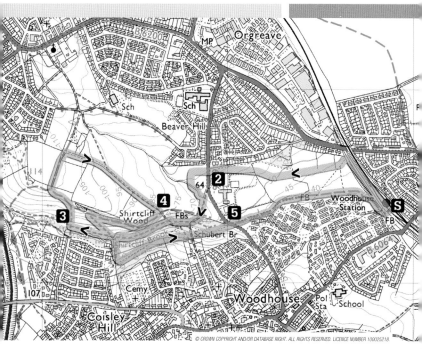

© CROWN COPYRIGHT AND/OR DATABASE RIGHT. ALL RIGHTS RESERVED. LICENCE NUMBER 100025218.

START Woodhouse railway station on Furnace Lane.

GRID REF SK 428854.

PARKING Woodhouse railway station.

PUBLIC TRANSPORT

Bus service 52 and 52a.

Train from Barnsley and Rotherham to Meadowhall then hourly to Woodhouse via Sheffield on the Retford and Lincoln line. On Sundays, due to a limited service, the bus from Sheffield is the better option.

TERRAIN Hilly, with one steep climb. Stout footwear recommended.

REFRESHMENTS The Junction, just above the station. (May not be open lunchtimes during the week.) *T* 0114 269 2648.

OS MAP Explorer 278, Sheffield, Barnsley and Rotherham, South sheet.

5 Shirtcliffe Wood from Flockton Park

S Descend the rough lane past the station and, just before reaching the road, turn **left** into Flockton Park. Leave the gravel path after 100m and turn **right** immediately beyond the trees. The building in the distance is a Fire Service training centre. Head to the **right** of this to Beaver Hill Road.

Shirtcliffe is typical ancient woodland, cloaking the slopes of a steep valley. Though the wood was mined for coal, the stream itself has never been dammed or used to provide water for industry, which is quite unique in Sheffield. The valley has a rich birdlife and varied flora, boasting thirteen ancient woodland indicators.

2 Cross to the gap opposite and follow the upper ride past houses. Curve **left** behind a line of trees, descend and turn **right** at the corner across a field into Shirtcliffe Wood. Descend the steps to Shirtcliffe Brook and turn **right** in front of the footbridge. There is a short stretch of boardwalk beyond the next bridge and a seat beyond the third. Exit the wood and stay by the stream to reach an obvious path junction.

3 Turn **right**, ascend steeply to the summit and turn **left**. Branch right after 100m onto a path between hedges. Continue 50m beyond the hedge and turn **right**. *(Excellent view from this path.)* Pass through a gap and continue with the hedge on your right past an old stone gatepost to the corner.

4 Go **straight ahead** and turn right at the path junction along the top edge of the wood. The path rises into the open along the scarp then through the wood to a stump that once supported a seat. Here, double back **left** and descend to re-enter Shirtcliffe Wood. Cross the plank footbridge and climb the hillside for 100m. After crossing a shallow ditch, turn **left** on a path marked by large daubs of yellow paint on two trees and follow these waymarkers, descending gradually to walk parallel with the stream. Beyond a seat the path descends to Beaver Hill Road.

Note the huge black poplar on the verge. This is a rare species and the biggest of its kind in the city.

5   Cross over, enter Flockton Park and continue by the stream. Pass through trees in the far left-hand corner and continue alongside them. Cross the gravel path and the one beyond to reach a footbridge. The improved path continues to Woodhouse station.

The Shirtcliffe Valley.

6 The Chapeltown Woods

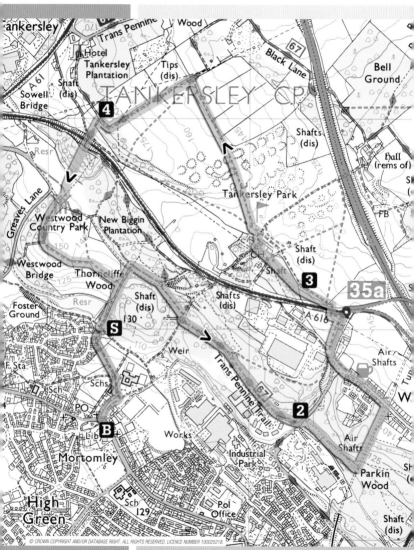

© CROWN COPYRIGHT AND/OR DATABASE RIGHT. ALL RIGHTS RESERVED. LICENCE NUMBER 100025218.

These woods, probably more than any others in the book, are most heavily scarred by the Industrial Revolution. Humps, hollows and old tips abound. Thankfully, the Trans Pennine Trail provides an easy route through. We also potter through the wilder fringes of Tankersley Park Golf Course and Westwood Country Park. Halfway refreshment is available in the village of Warren.

START Westwood Gate car park at Thorncliffe Reservoir, High Green.
GRID REF SK 343980 (car park) / SK 337977 (Thompson Hill) / SK 343976 (Ecclesfield Parish Council offices).
PARKING Westwood Gate. *To reach the car park from High Green, turn off Wortley Road along Westwood Road, which is opposite the junction with Thompson Hill. Turn right on Dowland Avenue. The car park is directly opposite the T-junction at the end.*
PUBLIC TRANSPORT
Bus services 1 and 1a. Service 66 from Rotherham to Chapeltown then the 1, 1a to High Green. *Train* from Barnsley to Chapeltown then the 1, 1a to High Green. *To reach the start of the walk from High Green, leave Mortomley Lane along Pack Horse Lane beside Ecclesfield Parish Council offices. Turn left through a metal barrier just beyond the Pack Horse car park, through an A-frame and straight on, across the end of a cul-de-sac to the car park.*

TERRAIN Mostly improved paths through the woods and good grassy paths over the golf course. Several short ascents.
REFRESHMENTS The Miners Arms in Warren. *T* 0114 245 9326.
OS MAP Explorer 278, Sheffield, Barnsley and Rotherham, South sheet.

6 The Chapeltown Woods

Thorncliffe Wood was decimated at the end of the 18th century with the building of the Newton and Chambers Ironworks, which by 1900 employed over 8,000 workers. Coal for the production of coke was mined alongside ironstone for the blast furnaces. A million tons of coal a year and a wide range of cast iron goods were produced and shipped out by rail. The branch lines now form the major tracks through the woods.

S From the entrance to the car park, turn **right** through the barrier and then immediately **left**. Cross a footbridge, climb the steps and ascend to meet the Trans Pennine Trail. Follow the improved path to the **right** through Thorncliffe Wood past a sign for High Green and over a path junction. The Trans Pennine Trail eventually runs between the wood and a modern industrial estate.

2 Cross the road into Parkin Wood (which has more seats than Wembley Stadium). Turn **left** beyond two seats close together, pass a low wooden barrier and ascend (quite surprisingly) past a seat. A stiff climb brings you out of the trees by a set of swings. Head down to the left-hand corner into Warren and turn **left** along the road. Fork **right** and cross to the junction. Ignore the signed Trans Pennine Trail route and take the bridleway through the A-frame and around the perimeter of the JCB offices. Cross the busy A616 and turn **left** along a faint path ascending the verge. This brings you to a metal kissing gate leading onto Tankersley Park Golf Course.

3 Pass below the 15th tee to a waymarker post behind the wooden fence opposite. The path through the wood is neglected but navigable and is preferred for safety's sake to the line shown on the OS Explorer, which runs along the edge of the fairway outside the wood. The golf course is busy at weekends and the possibility of being struck should be avoided. Pass to the **left** of the building and take the wider of the two waymarked paths past the hut overlooking the 14th tee. Pass the clubhouse and continue along the cinder track.

6.5 km / 4 miles

When this ends, cross the fairway and pass the 5th tee to join a wall on your right. The path eventually leaves the edge of the fairway and meanders through the rough to the 6th tee. Turn **left** at a post and join the Barnsley Boundary Walk, the right-hand of two waymarked paths. This heads for and follows a line of overhead cables through the wooded fringe alongside the fairway.

4 Pass a barrier, cross the wooden stile, descend and turn **left** to cross the footbridge over the A616. Ignore the bridleway dipping left and go straight on along a grassy ride. This becomes a cinder path descending into Westwood Country Park, home to the Concorde Model Flying Club, and busy on fine weekends.

Head down to the footpath sign at the corner of the wood and go straight on through the barrier. Climb up into the open, cross a stile and turn **left** alongside a fence. There are views over High Green to your right and the Chapeltown woods in front. Continue to descend on the main path and bear **right** at the fork. Rejoin your outward path back to the car park.

A serious riot took place adjacent to the reservoir in 1870 when armed strikers attacked a double row of miner's cottages occupied by non-union members. Police reinforcements from Barnsley were needed to quell the rioting and violence. Twenty-three men were sent for trial and soldiers were moved into the area for the next six months to keep the peace.

Parkin Wood.

7 Eckington Woods

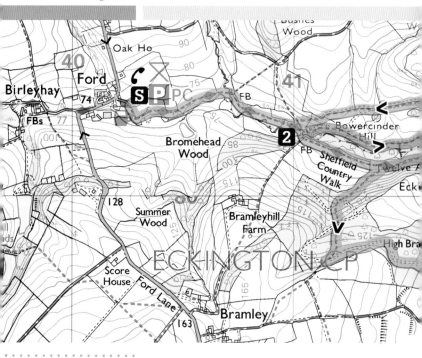

The woods lining the lower Moss Valley are mainly commercial forests, yet are varied and have an excellent network of paths. Much of the outward route is through the woods, with the return more open with views of this beautiful valley. Walk 12 (p48) starts from the same car park and explores the valley in the other direction.

8 km / 5 miles

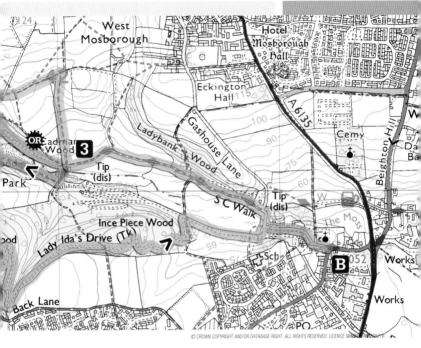

© CROWN COPYRIGHT AND/OR DATABASE RIGHT. ALL RIGHTS RESERVED. LICENCE NUMBER 100048218.

START Car park adjacent to Ford dam, next to the Bridge Inn, Birleyhay.

GRID REF SK 402804.

PARKING Ford dam.

PUBLIC TRANSPORT

Bus service 252 (TM Travel) from Sheffield, Eckington or Crystal Peaks. No Sunday service. *Train* from Rotherham and Barnsley. Hourly Sunday service 50 to Eckington church and join the route at Ladybank Wood.

TERRAIN Some moderate ascents. Stout footwear recommended.

REFRESHMENTS The Bridge Inn, Birleyhay. Open all day for real ale and food. *T* 01246 433217.

OS MAP OS Explorer 278, Sheffield, Barnsley and Rotherham, South sheet; and OS Explorer 269, Chesterfield and Alfreton.

7 Eckington Woods

During the 19th century the Moss Valley supported a thriving agricultural industry. Water-powered tilt hammer forges produced scythes and sickles for export to developing countries all over the world.

S Take the path around the right-hand side of Ford dam, following the River Moss. Cross a tributary and stay on the riverside path to pass another fishing pond.

2 Cross the footbridge over the Moss and continue along the field edge into Twelve Acre Wood. Double back **right** after 100m and climb the broad path up out of the valley. Turn **left** at the T-junction at the top, pass an opening on the right and stay with the track inside High Bramley Wood. Bear **left** at the junction near a house and, at the waymarked fork, double back **sharply right** along Lady Ida's Drive. This rounds the head of an unnamed stream and continues just inside the southern boundary.

Cross a public footpath entering from the right and continue into Ince Piece Wood. The path divides at a bend but soon reunites. Descend to a T-junction and turn **right** along the main track leading out of the wood. Follow this **left** to a metal barrier and turn **left** along the road past a small weir to another barrier. Follow the fence on your left for 1km through Ladybank Wood and on to Cadman Wood.

Lady Ida was the wife of Sir George Reresby Sitwell of Renishaw Hall, a stately home and gardens near Eckington. Their three children, Edith, Osbert and Sacheverell all became famous writers.

3 Continue a few metres past a waymarked fork to a path junction (footbridge to your left) – turn **right** and ascend the field. Cross the stile and continue up the grassy path ahead, which rounds the hillside to a stile. Turn **left** alongside the hedge, cross a bridleway and fork **left**. The path goes left into trees to a stile. Follow the fence on your left through two pastures into an arable field and descend through the wood to the pond at point **2**.

OPTIONAL ROUTE

From here you can retrace your steps back to the car park, **or** add 2.5km by doubling back to the metal stile on the left bank of the Moss. Leave the wood and follow the field-edge. Ascend to a stile, turn **right** down into the wood and rejoin the river, which you follow intermittently back to point **3**. Cross the footbridge, turn **right** at the T-junction and continue into Twelve Acre Wood, past the turnoff and on to the car park.

The Moss Valley.

8 Glen Howe Park & More Hall Reservoir

© CROWN COPYRIGHT AND/OR DATABASE RIGHT. ALL RIGHTS RESERVED. LICENCE NUMBER 100025218.

8 km / 5 miles

We walk through ornamental ancient woodland, meadows and beside open water to a high-level picnic spot with a great view before returning to the park.

More Hall Reservoir.

START Glen Howe Park, Wharncliffe Side, which is signposted from the A6102 via Green Lane.
GRID REF SK 296943.
PARKING Glen Howe Park.
PUBLIC TRANSPORT
Bus services 57 (not Sundays) and SL (Super Tram Link) from Middlewood Park & Ride.
Train from Rotherham and Barnsley to Meadowhall then *tram* to Middlewood Park & Ride and Tramlink bus. *Walk*

up Green Lane and continue along the roughly surfaced track at the bend into Glen Howe Park.
TERRAIN A strenuous walk with a number of hills. Stout footwear recommended.
REFRESHMENTS Wharncliffe Arms in Wharncliffe Side. *T* 0114 286 4659.
OS MAP OS Explorer 278, Sheffield, Barnsley and Rotherham, South sheet; or OS Explorer 1, The Peak District, Dark Peak area – East sheet.

8 Glen Howe Park & More Hall Reservoir

Mills later added a tea pavilion and landscaped the wood into a pleasure garden for visitors. Mills and his benefactor, Joseph Dixon, the manager of a local paper mill, presented the park to the people of Wharncliffe Side in 1917. It passed to Sheffield City Council in 1971 and was restored under Fuelling a Revolution.

S Follow the lane past the toilets to Glen Howe Tower, built in 1881 by stonemason, John Mills. Go **left** beyond the house and climb the steps through the wood to an open area. *The circular enclosure, named the Tobhta Stone Shelter, was built by sculptor Ian Boyle.* Turn **right** and follow the lower path into the wood. Pass a restored timber shelter, branch **right** and descend to cross the packhorse bridge.

Built in 1734, the bridge originally stood beside a corn mill on Ewden Beck. Joseph Dixon bought and dismantled it in 1925 whilst More Hall Reservoir was under construction. It was rebuilt in 1929.

2 Ascend the first stepped zigzag path (without rails) to a stile and rise into the meadow to join a wall on the right. Pass to the **left** of Swinnock Hall and along the farm track. Turn **right** and **right** again into the hamlet of Brightholmlee. Turn **left** on the footpath to Lee Farm, 50m beyond the water troughs dated 1886. Enter a path between walls, cross a meadow and descend through mixed woodland to More Hall Reservoir. Join the shoreline and follow it all the way to New Mill Bridge.

This waymarked Yorkshire Water permissive path has a number of benches early on, and is a pleasant spot for a short break, with a grand view towards the dam.

3 Turn **left**, pass the signed track into Horse Wood and continue for 100m to the next footpath sign by an electricity pylon. Bear **right** towards the house and remain close by the fence and wall to a stone stile. Continue to climb alongside the tiny stream and turn **right** along the track, but leave it at a stile on the **left** just before reaching a road. Ascend **left** into the pathless field and head for a stile in the far corner, using the quarry spoil heap on the hillside ahead as a guide. Follow the wall/fence to a stile. Descend to a footbridge spanning a tumbling beck and climb up to the road at Snell House.

Turn **right** and, where the stream issues from beneath a stone parapet, branch **left** to a squeezer and ascend steeply alongside the wall. Once in the field above, head up to the right to join a track at a waymarked pillar and turn **left**.

Continue along the track and, when it peters out, head over to the **right** on a bearing to the left of the radio mast. Bear **left** as you approach the spoil heaps to the metal gate in the wall, which has a waymarker on the gatepost. Hop over the rough stile, close with the broken wall, admiring the view as you proceed. Cross the ditch where it shallows and continue with the wall to a sunken farm track. Follow this to Spout House Farm, pass through a gate and bear **right** down the track.

4 Cross the stile beside Tinker Brook House and descend past the pond to join the stream. Cross the footbridge and stile, leave the fence at the signpost and continue towards the farm. Turn **left** along the road, pass through the gate and follow the waymarkers to the **right** of the houses. After 50m leave the road and turn **left** into fields and continue to descend, entering Glen Howe Park at a wall stile.

Take the left-hand path, which curves **left** past a seat. Just beyond, keep **right** and descend to a fence – a viewpoint overlooking Tinker Brook. Continue down to a junction and turn **left**. Bear **right** in front of the packhorse bridge through an open area with seats and a stone bird sculpture, the work of a former resident of Glen Howe Tower. Cross the footbridge by a triangular seat built around a birch tree. Turn **right** then **left**, with Tinker Brook now on your right. Continue to a footbridge leading back to the road near the toilets and turn **left** back to the car park.

After all your hard work, you deserve a view, and they don't come much better than this. On your left near the top, and directly above the rocks, is a flat area of grass perfect for a picnic.

9 New Hall Wood & Whitwell Moor

A walk of great contrasts, featuring urban woodland in Stocksbridge, the wild open heights of Whitwell Moor and a stroll along the bank of Underbank reservoir. Stocksbridge has now become an officially recognised 'Walkers are Welcome' town.

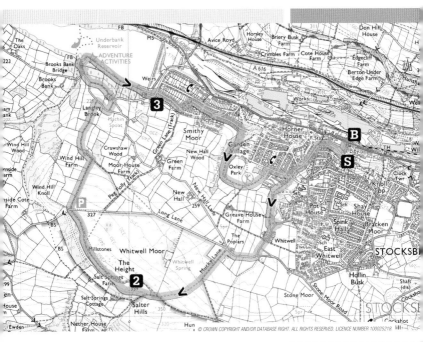

START Stocksbridge Co-op.
GRID REF SK 269985.
PARKING The car park at the top of Johnson Street, signposted from the main road, up by the side of the Co-op.
PUBLIC TRANSPORT
Bus services 57 (not Sundays) and SL (Super Tram Link) from Middlewood Park & Ride. Service 23 from Barnsley every two hours (not Sundays).
Train from Rotherham and Barnsley to Meadowhall then *tram* to Middlewood Park & Ride and Tramlink bus.
TERRAIN The ascent and descent are long but relatively gentle. Stout footwear is recommended for this high level walk over moorland.
REFRESHMENTS Plenty in Stocksbridge.
OS MAP OS Explorer OL1, The Peak District, Dark Peak area – East sheet.

9 New Hall Wood & Whitwell Moor

S Turn **right** at the top of Johnson Street along Edward Street and cross over into Coronation Road. At the far end, continue up Viola Bank, enter Pot House Wood and ascend the tarmac path on the **right**. Follow the driveway and turn **right** along the lane past Whitwell Farm to a junction. Turn **right**, then **left** at the footpath sign along the quaintly named Mucky Lane, which leads to access land. A clear grassy path, which can be wet underfoot, rises over moorland and pasture. Pass through the gateway to the **right** of the gravel path and head up to the trig point on the summit.

Pause here at what is now a memorial and take in the stunning 360° vista. Whitwell Moor is one of many areas to benefit from the CRoW Act of 2000, which allows open access for walkers on mountain, moor, heath, down and common land.

2 From the trig point, gradually rejoin the path on the other side of the wall. The surface becomes improved as you reach the trees, which can also provide welcome relief from the wind. Cross Long Lane to the stile beside the information panel and descend alongside the wall to the bottom corner.

Turn **left** through Wind Hill Farm and descend the enclosed path to a lane – turn **right**. After 200m turn **left** at a footpath sign and descend the field to the right of the wall. Turn **left**, as directed, along a track and pass to the **right** of the farm into an enclosed woodland path. Turn **right** down the lane and right again through Underbank car park. Pass through an A-frame towards the outdoor activity centre. Turn **right** beyond the climbing wall along the southern shore of the reservoir.

Underbank is the third in the trio of reservoirs mentioned on Walk 30 (p138). The activity centre is run by Sheffield City Council and is ideally situated to combine water activities like canoeing and sailing with woodland-based activities like orienteering and rope climbs.

3   Continue into Cross Lane and turn **left** at the footpath sign opposite Green Lane. Turn **right** at the cul de sac and follow Churchill Road past Newton Lane. Branch **right** into Hawthorne Avenue and enter New Hall Wood beyond the last house. After 20m branch **left** down into the valley bottom and follow the path sharply to the **right** alongside the stream, which becomes a little livelier above a small dam. Climb the steps and turn **right** along a tarmac path. This climbs out of the wood and circuits Oxley Park. Pass through the Leisure Centre car park and turn **right** along Alpine Road. At the bottom of the dip turn **left** back down Viola Bank and return along Coronation Road and Edward Street to the start.

Memorial trig point on Whitwell Moor.

10 Wheata Wood & Birley Edge

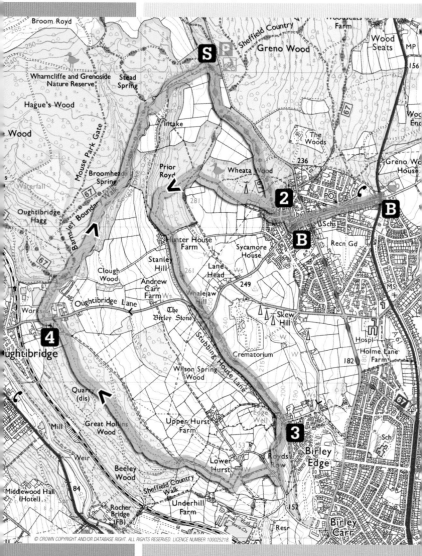

9 km / 5.5 miles

This walk features two Fuelling a Revolution woods, but the highlight is the traverse of Birley Edge, which affords great views across the city and surrounding countryside. It can be extended by 5km by adding on Walk 2 Prior Royd and Birkin Royd (p8), which starts from the same point, but explores the area to the north.

START Greno Wood car park on Woodhead Road, 800m north of Grenoside.

GRID REF SK 324951.

PARKING Greno Wood car park.

PUBLIC TRANSPORT

Bus services 85 to the Old Harrow Inn. Service 66 from Rotherham to Chapeltown then 86. *Train* from Barnsley to Chapeltown, then 86. *The 86 stops on the main A61 by the Norfolk Arms. Walk up Norfolk Hill to the crossroads by the Old Harrow Inn and go straight on along Stephen Lane.*

Take the public footpath on the right after 100m. Turn left, pass an ancient water trough and at Middle Lane turn right on the Trans Pennine Trail signed Wortley. Branch left at the notice board and again to join the route at point 2.

TERRAIN Two prolonged ascents. Stout footwear is essential for this walk, as you will encounter a short stretch of farmyard mud at most times of the year.

REFRESHMENTS Pubs in Grenoside and on the A61.

OS MAP Explorer 278, Sheffield, Barnsley and Rotherham, South sheet.

10 Wheata Wood & Birley Edge

The ancient coppice of Wheata Wood was surrounded by walls to prevent deer and livestock grazing the young trees.

S Head south with Woodhead Road on your left and follow the Trans Pennine Trail to Grenoside.

2 Leave the Trans Pennine Trail at a noticeboard 100m before reaching the houses. The improved path immediately forks **left** through a wide gap in a wooden fence and heads west through the fringe of the wood. Enter Prior Royd, ignore all path junctions and continue downhill. The path curves **left** past a seat, where the forest has been thinned to provide a view over Wharncliffe Woods and the Don Valley to the moors beyond. Turn first **left** at the T-junction and follow the upper path to a double stile. Continue ahead along the scarp with Oughtibridge on your right and Hillsborough ahead. The path ascends to run alongside the wall. This wild hillside is particularly colourful in August when the heather is in bloom. Cross the road to the Birley Stone, a medieval boundary marker, beside which is a topograph, erected in 1951, and continue along the ridge. Further along, the blue-painted stands of Sheffield Wednesday FC come into view with the Hallamshire Hospital and Sheffield University Arts Tower prominent beyond.

3 Cross the road, but don't continue along the edge. Take the grassy path on the **right** before the first of three large boulders. Descend fairly steeply and bear **left** at the junction. Ignore the stone stile on your right and continue along the bottom of the wood to a road and turn **right**. Turn **left** beyond Lapwater Cottage and ascend the field. Turn **right** into the farmyard and immediately **sharp left** alongside the wall. The field is liable to be churned and muddy. Cross diagonally to a stile beside the gate in the right-hand corner. An enclosed path leads into Beeley Wood just after passing beneath an electricity pylon. Ignore the path on the right and enter the wood. Branch immediately **right**, pass a shallow quarry and fork **right** at a red brick structure. Pass beneath overhead wires and continue through the more mature Great Hollins Wood. Towards the end, cross a track to reach Oughtibridge Lane and turn **left**.

4 After 50m turn **right** along a concrete drive and, when this bends left, continue on the Trans Pennine Trail. Pass through an A-frame into Wharncliffe Woods, a large area of mixed woodland that is both a commercial forest owned by the Forestry Commission and a nature reserve. Leave the Trans Pennine Trail and follow Sough Dike. The track ascends fairly steeply, rejoins the Trans Pennine Trail and immediately branches **right** along a short red cinder path. You eventually cross Broomhead Spring and pass a bridleway on the right. Where two paths leave the Trans Pennine Trail, take the first one, which crosses a wooden footbridge. Bear **left** to the far corner and join a stony track. This rises into open pasture; at its end cross the stile at the end of the wall, climb the steps and turn **right** for the car park. For the bus continue along the Trans Pennine Trail to Grenoside.

11 The Gleadless Valley Woods

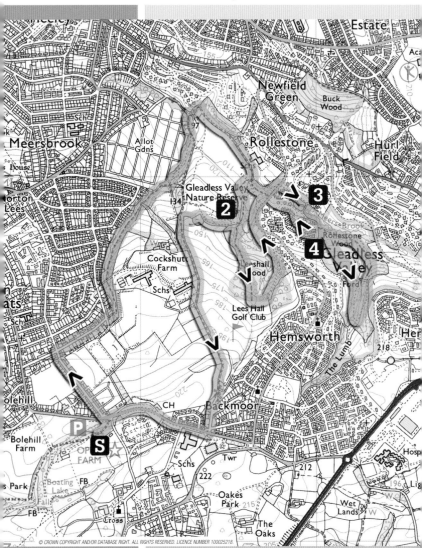

© CROWN COPYRIGHT AND/OR DATABASE RIGHT. ALL RIGHTS RESERVED. LICENCE NUMBER 100025218.

This outing wins the prize for the most Fuelling a Revolution woods in a single walk; a total of five. We start from Graves Park, which gives you the opportunity to visit the Animal Farm, park, café and a pub. Graves Park was presented to the city by Alderman Grace between 1925 and 1936. At over 200 acres, it is Sheffield's largest park and has much to interest the walker.

START Graves Park Animal Farm.
The farm, which is home to rare and domestic breeds of farm animals and birds, is free and well worth a visit.
GRID REF SK 358826.
PARKING Inexpensive Pay and Display car park at Graves Park Animal Farm.
PUBLIC TRANSPORT
Bus services 20. *Train* from Rotherham and Barnsley.

TERRAIN Mostly improved paths through woodland.
REFRESHMENTS New Inn, Hemsworth Road, very near the end of the walk, *T* 0114 255 4436; and the café in Graves Park, *T* 0114 258 2705. *The farm and timber-framed café by the Rose Garden are open 10am – 4pm, and there are toilets at the café.*
OS MAP Explorer 278, Sheffield, Barnsley and Rotherham, South sheet.

11 The Gleadless Valley Woods

Like all the woods visited today, Ashes is ancient coppiced woodland, which produced charcoal for the iron and steel industry, and whitecoal for lead smelting. The steepness of the valley made it unsuitable for agricultural use during the original clearances and protected it from urban sprawl.

S Cross Hemsworth Road and walk down Warminster Road. Turn **right** along Mount View Road to its junction with Woodland Road and take the footpath opposite. Cross the stream and turn **left** into Ashes Wood. Descend the steps, pass under the flyover and continue above the stream, which you eventually join. Joining a wider path, cross the stream on stepping stones and bear **right** over a footbridge into Carr Wood. Keep to the main path, ignoring side paths left and right, to reach a green post by a seat. Take the **left** fork and descend past a seat overlooking the steep valley. Turn **right** at the junction beyond Rose Cottage into Hang Bank Wood, ascend beside the stream and turn **right** at the junction by the exit. Keep **left** with the main path, pass a barrier on your right and continue along the woodland edge, through an A-frame and past a school. Cross the bridge and road in front of the recycling centre and enter Leeshall Wood. Cross over the stream, ascend and turn **left**.

2 Carry on over a path junction and ascend. Take either the central or right-hand path past a corner of the golf course to reach a fence at the edge of the wood. Turn **left** down steps and cross three plank footbridges to a junction where the golf course fence ends. Bear **left** to reach a seat, descend **right** over a stream and turn **left**. Bear **left** at the next seat in 50m (deep valley to your left), pass through an A-frame and descend to a fork by some steps. Bear **right** and maintain height to meet Blackstock Road at an A-frame opposite the Horse & Groom. Cross the flyover and turn **right** into the road. Descend the steps to continue alongside the railings.

3   Turn **right** at the A-frame and then **left** beyond the bridge into Rollestone Wood. Join an improved path and bear right at the fork after 150m. This partially cleared area has many fallen trunks left to nature. Note the new growth coming through. Fork **left** at a seat and cross the stream. The path follows the left bank for a while and then ascends to a fork a few metres before a bridge. Rise to the **left**, pass a flight of steps and continue to a T-junction. Turn **left** downhill to merge with another improved path at a seat. Continue over a bridge to complete the circuit of Rollestone Wood and retrace your steps beside Meers Brook.

4   Leave the wood at the ornamental barrier and turn **right** alongside railings. Pass under the flyover and turn **left**. Re-cross the bridge into Leeshall Wood and follow your earlier route as far as the cross-path (point **2**). Bear **right** and ascend the tarmac, keeping **right** when it becomes an improved path. Turn **left** at the junction past a small pond and fork **left** beside the golf course boundary fence. Follow this path south for 1.2km to the New Inn on Hemsworth Road and turn **right** back to the car park.

Meers Brook, despite its size, is one of the most historic boundaries in Britain. It separated the Anglo Saxon kingdoms of Northumbria and Mercia, then the counties of Yorkshire and Derbyshire, before finally being relegated to the parish boundary between Norton and Handsworth. Now its north and south banks even have the same postcode. How the mighty have fallen!

12 The Upper Moss Valley

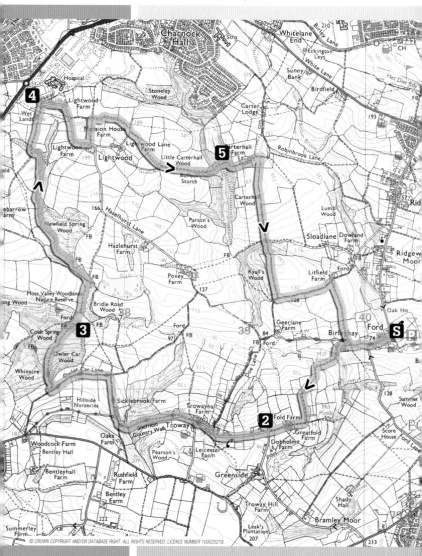

© CROWN COPYRIGHT AND/OR DATABASE RIGHT. ALL RIGHTS RESERVED. LICENCE NUMBER 100025218.

Drive beyond Wetlands.

The ancient woods on this walk, which starts from the same place as Walk 7 (p28), are managed by Sheffield Wildlife Trust. The views are excellent and the woods are particularly beautiful during the bluebell season.

START Car park adjacent to Ford dam, next to the Bridge Inn, Birleyhay.
GRID REF SK 402804.
PARKING Ford dam.
PUBLIC TRANSPORT
Bus service 252 TM Travel from Sheffield, Eckington or Crystal Peaks. No Sunday service. *Train* from Rotherham and Barnsley. *Tram* from city centre to Herdings/Leighton Road and footpath to join the route at point **4** (1.5km).

TERRAIN A hilly walk on natural paths. Stout footwear recommended.
REFRESHMENTS The Gate Inn, Troway. No food, but a Good Beer Guide pub. *T* 01246 413280; The Bridge Inn, Birleyhay. Open all day for real ale and food. *T* 01246 433217.
OS MAP OS Explorer 278, Sheffield, Barnsley and Rotherham, South sheet; and OS Explorer 269, Chesterfield and Alfreton.

12 The Upper Moss Valley

The lake down to your right is the legacy of the scythe and sickle manufacturing industry that thrived in the Moss Valley in the 19th century. It supplied water to power tilt hammer forges.

S Cross the picnic area, pass through the pub car park and turn **left**. Branch **right** at the bend then **left** along the Private Road. Follow the drive through Birleyhay and ascend **right** alongside a fence. Cross the stile, continue to the corner and turn **left**. Pass through a gate after 80m and ascend to a waymarked gateway. The track bends right past Fold Farm, which bears the date 1687 above the door. The views open up over the Moss Valley to Norton Water Tower.

Owler Car Wood, together with Cook Spring Wood and Nor Wood, was purchased by The Woodland Trust from the Sitwell Estate in 1988. All the woods in the vicinity are managed by Sheffield Wildlife Trust for nature conservation and public access.

2 Join the road, continue into Troway and go straight on over a stile at the bend beyond the Gate Inn. The view to the right is even broader as you progress along a grassy path and through the first of today's woods. Cross Sickle Brook and bear **right** on a rising path. Turn **right**, and **right** again, past Sicklebrook Farm along an improved bridleway to Owler Car Lane – turn **left** here. Pass a gas pumping station and enter Owler Car Wood through a gate at the far side. Pass through the lower gap in a wooden fence and descend through the wood (public footpath waymark).

3 Descend the steps, cross the River Moss and climb into a clearing. A few metres beyond the stile, branch **right** over a stile into Bridle Road Wood. At the far end, ignore the footbridge and turn **left** along the field edge for 50m. Enter Newfield Spring Wood at a stile and follow the valley for 1km. At a fork, bear **right** down the slope and cross an unbridged tributary. (The left fork leaves the wood at a stile in 50m.) You pass a shallow hollow on your right with another just to the left. These were probably White Coal Hearths or Q pits, where charcoal was burnt to smelt lead. Cross a plank footbridge and continue up to the **left**. Pass under overhead wires at the end of a field, advance a few metres to a fork and bear **right** down the slope to a gate. Ascend through a gap in the hedge and continue over two ladder stiles along the drive of Wetlands.

4 Turn **right** and follow the lane around two bends to a stone stile on the **left** just past Lightwood Farm. Follow the hedge around to a stile and turn **right**. Turn **right** at the junction then immediately **left**. Veer away from the hedge to a signpost in the hedge and bear **right** along the edge of the next field. Turn **left** at the waymarker post into an avenue of trees and bear slightly **left** at the next waymarker alongside the trees on your right. At the bottom of the dip turn **right** down steps into Carterhall Wood. Descend to cross a stream and fork **right** up to and over a path junction.

Though the most isolated of the woods on this walk, Carterhall is, in my humble opinion, the finest bluebell wood in the area. You can explore it more fully in the spring by using the path that runs north-south the length of the wood.

5 The climb is steep and winding with intermittent steps. Cross pasture to a redundant stile and continue alongside the hedge. Cross a stone stile on your **right** at the end of a wooden fence and follow the hedge over the brow and down a long field. Enter Ryall's Wood and go straight on to a waymarker post in 50m. Ascend into the field and follow the hedge to a T-junction. Turn **left** along an enclosed bridleway. This eventually widens and descends to the residential Litfield Farm complex. Turn **right** through a gap in the hedge by a waymarker post and complete the descent to the houses in the valley bottom via two stiles. Bear **left** along the lane and road back to the start.

13 Bowden Housteads & Tinsley Park Woods

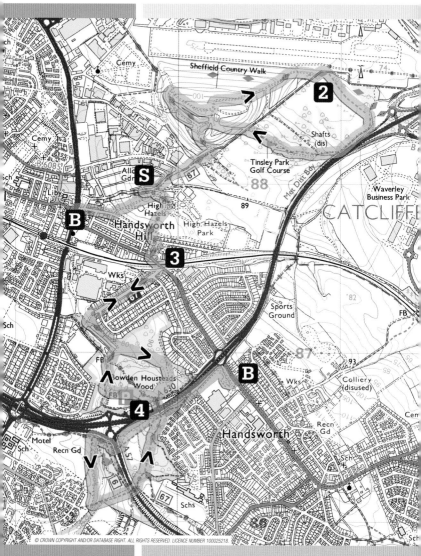

© CROWN COPYRIGHT AND/OR DATABASE RIGHT. ALL RIGHTS RESERVED. LICENCE NUMBER 100025218.

This figure-of-eight walk can be split into two. The Fuelling a Revolution woods that are the focus of the walk are only a mile apart and linked by the Trans Pennine Trail, which is signposted through the quiet residential area separating them. The 4km Tinsley Park loop crosses a golf course and reclaimed colliery land with stunning views, whilst the 7.25km circuit through Bowden Housteads includes High Hazels Park and a local nature reserve.

START High Hazels Park, signposted (along with Tinsley Park golf course) from the A6102, Greenland Road.

GRID REF SK 398879.

PARKING High Hazels Park. Note the car park for High Hazels is just beyond the golf club car park.

PUBLIC TRANSPORT

There are two start points for this walk: *Bus services* 52 and 52a to the junction of Greenland Road and Main Street, Darnall (Grid ref: SK 394878). *Cross Greenland Road at the lights, turn left then first right along Senior Road. Enter High Hazels Park and turn left after 80m up the hill. Branch left and leave the park at the yellow barrier at the top.* *Bus services* 52, 52a, X5 and 30 stop

at Asda on Handsworth Road (Grid ref: SK 403868). *A walkway descends to a slip road on the far side of the car park opposite the supermarket entrance. Take the tarmac path through the A-frame into Bowden Housteads Wood to join the route at point 4 where a footbridge crosses the Parkway.* Service 72 from Rotherham to Asda or 27 and 29 to Swallownest then service X5 to Asda. *Train* from Barnsley.

TERRAIN Mostly improved paths and some road walking.

REFRESHMENTS None (unless brave enough to sit in Asda café in your hiking gear!).

OS MAP Explorer 278, Sheffield, Barnsley and Rotherham, South sheet.

13 Bowden Housteads & Tinsley Park Woods

S Turn **right** out of High Hazels car park and go straight on at the bend. Turn **left** through the A-frame, **left** again at the statue by the pond and branch **right** off the Trans Pennine Trail up the hill. Excellent views open up across the Don Valley. Bear **right** alongside the fence and continue to climb. The city centre and the moors beyond come into view to your right. *You are crossing the site of Tinsley Park Colliery, which closed in 1943.* Continue ahead through the gate at the junction, with the view from the highest point now ranging over Rotherham and Canklow Wood. The path descends and continues to the **right**.

The house was built in 1850 by William Jeffcock, the first Lord Mayor of Sheffield. It became a recreational park in 1895. Numerous improvements were made following the formation of The Friends of High Hazels Park in 1998.

2 Turn **left** beyond the barrier and follow the fence around the corner. After 150m, turn **right** into the wood. The path climbs level alongside the Parkway and then bears **right** between fairways past the 16th tee to meet the Trans Pennine Trail. Continue along the permissive bridleway and turn **left** past the pond to retrace your steps to High Hazels Park. Follow the Trans Pennine Trail into the park and down past the children's playground to the bottom of the hill. Continue **left** (signed *Handsworth*), **right** up Olivers Drive and **left** at Handsworth Road.

The ascending path is lined with seats funded by the Fuelling a Revolution programme. Note how the area on your right looks random and natural (good management), whereas on the left the oak and beech trees have been allowed to grow to the same size, spreading a dense canopy that has inhibited the under layer (poor management).

3 Cross at the lights and turn **right** into Handsworth Avenue. Pass through the barrier at the far end and immediately bear **left** off the tarmac. Enter Bowden Housteads through an A-frame and after 50m turn **left** just before the next Trans Pennine Trail sign. The path levels and meets a diagonal path at a junction – turn **right** (there are houses to the left and a seat just beyond the turning). Turn **right** at a T-junction and, after a few metres, fork to the **left**.

4 Cross the bridge over the Parkway and turn **right** past the strongly-muscled sculpture of the Steel Giant, the work of local sculptor Jason Thomson. Fork **left** to cross Mosborough Parkway, turn **right** and stay with the tarmac path across the head of a valley to a T-junction. Double back **left** past a barrier and along the valley bottom beside the stream. Follow the railings past a pond and pick up the stream again close to a colourful pipeline. Cross a concrete bridge further on and turn **left** at the top of the slope. Pass through an A-frame into the meadows of a local nature reserve and branch **left** along the top of Car Brook Ravine. Branch **right** through the gap at the end of the hedge and ascend the hill. Cross the A57, turn **left** along the Trans Pennine Trail back into Bowden Housteads and bear **left** at the fork.

OPTIONAL ROUTE

In summer I recommend crossing the low barrier on your **left** at this point to explore an area of heath, which is slowly being re-colonised by heather, wild flowers and young trees. Follow the faint path to a reverse fork and turn **right** to rejoin the Trans Pennine Trail. You can see from the numerous stumps that this part of the wood has been thinned to allow light to penetrate the canopy.

Re-cross the Parkway and turn **left** at the end of the tarmac. Turn **left** at the cross-path then **right** at the seat to join a streambed. Before turning **right** at the junction, descend to the boardwalk and just beyond to view the wet crack willow woodland where the dry tributary joins the permanent stream of Car Brook. Rejoin the Trans Pennine Trail and follow it **left** out of the wood at the point you came in. Retrace your steps back along the Trans Pennine Trail to High Hazels Park or catch a bus from Handsworth Road.

Bowden Housteads is one of the oldest surviving woods in Sheffield, documented since 1332. It was regularly coppiced and replanted from the 16th to the 19th centuries before passing to Sheffield Corporation in 1916. Much of it was lost to opencast mining in the 1940s, and again when Sheffield Parkway was built in 1970 and Mosborough Parkway in 1990.

Rotherham

The Rotherham walks are a mixture of ancient woodland, industrial archaeology and visitor attractions. Featuring walks to Roche Abbey, Catcliffe Glass Cone, the Waterloo Pottery Kiln, the Chesterfield Canal and England's largest stately home – Wentworth Woodhouse – combined with beautiful meadowland and some of the finest *Fuelling a Revolution* woods in the county, these walks offer a refreshing break from urban life.

Keppel's Column. PHOTO: David Coefield

Roche Abbey.

14 Canklow Wood Heritage Trail

Fuelling a Revolution waymarker.

This is the Fuelling a Revolution flagship walk. It is the only one that is specifically waymarked, and it is dotted with strategically-placed interpretive panels. Canklow Wood covers a large area, is riddled with paths and merits wider exploration on a return visit.

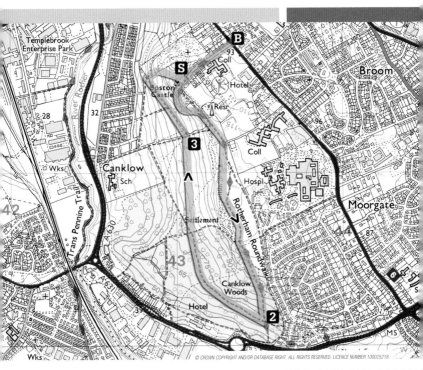

START Boston Park, off Moorgate.
GRID REF SK 431915.
PARKING Boston Castle.
PUBLIC TRANSPORT
Bus services 10, 27 and 29. *Alight
at Thomas Rotherham College on
Moorgate and walk up Boston Castle
Grove.* **Train** from Sheffield and
Barnsley.

TERRAIN Mostly natural paths.
REFRESHMENTS Boston Castle
(when open).
OS MAP Explorer 278, Sheffield,
Barnsley and Rotherham, South sheet.

14 Canklow Wood Heritage Trail

Boston Castle was built in 1775 as a shooting lodge for the Earl of Effingham, who supported the American colonialists against the British in a dispute over the Tea Act of 1773, which allowed the East India Company to undercut their colonial rivals and monopolise the market. In retaliation, a group called the Sons of Liberty raided three company-owned ships moored in Boston Harbour and dumped 45 tons of tea in the water. The event became known as the Boston Tea Party.

Despite the industrial foreground, the view from the castle is splendid. The black buildings of the Magna centre and the green roofs of Meadowhall stand out, with Sheffield nestling beyond Tinsley Park.

The renovated lodge is open to the public Tuesday, Wednesday, Saturday and Sunday 11am to 3pm from April to September. Admission is free and there are toilets and limited refreshments.

S Pass between boulders onto the swathe of grass, which narrows to a footpath running along the edge. Join a tarmac path beyond the old Bowling Green and follow this to a T-junction. Turn **right** through an A-frame beside the masts and enter Canklow Wood. Pass the first of 15 interpretive panels (some of which have disappeared) and bear **right** at the fork, where you encounter the first Fuelling a Revolution waymark; a ragged yellow arrow in a green circle. Divert **right** at the next waymark to a mostly overgrown viewpoint, minus its information panel. Rejoin the main path, pass a multi-stemmed oak tree and fork **left** on a natural path. Cross an improved path and branch **right** before reaching the houses. Pass panel 5 and descend.

2 In a small open area, just before the path narrows between holly bushes, look for a path going **right** (the broken waymark post may still be lodged upside down in the cleft of a tree). Follow the higher path and in 100m you should pick up a Fuelling a Revolution waymark, soon followed by panel 7. Fork to the **right** of this past panels 8, 9 and 10. Pass a redundant stile and enter a more open area of birch scrub. (*Before turning* **right** *at panel 12, I recommend going straight across for 70m to view the heath, which is being restored to preserve the heather.*) Pass panel 13 and turn **left** at the junction by panel 14 (uprooted).

3 Cross a wall just beyond the final panel (uprooted) and turn **right**. Ignore the official route going straight up the slope back into the park and take the **left** fork. Keep **left** on the less-worn path, cross the tarmac and keep to the contour through meadowland. The view is more open and less restricted than from above. Maintain height at a grassy fork by a boulder. The thin path appears to be going nowhere, but it curves **right** and climbs to pass the edge of a cemetery with a great view from which to while away eternity. Ascend the steps into an open area and turn **right** for the car park or left down Boston Castle Grove for the bus.

Boston Park.

Firsby Nature Reserve.

An attractive walk, almost entirely on permissive paths, exploring a deep valley lined with fishing ponds. An optional 2km extension around the Firsby Reservoirs Local Nature Reserve is included.

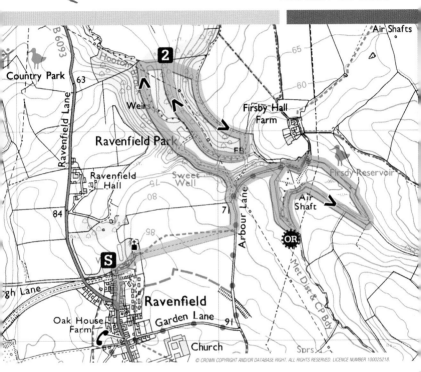

START St James Church, Ravenfield. Leave the B6093 along Church Lane.

GRID REF SK 485954.

PARKING At the bottom of Church Lane, or 50m further on.

PUBLIC TRANSPORT

Bus service Infrequent service 13, TM Travel. Four buses a day, two on Saturdays.

Train from Sheffield and Barnsley.

TERRAIN A fairly strenuous walk with a couple of short, stiff climbs, on mostly natural paths.

REFRESHMENTS None.

OS MAP Explorer 279, Doncaster, South sheet.

15 Ravenfield Park

Created as a deer park by the Westby family in the 15th century, Ravenfield is now home to an angling club. Access is provided through DEFRA, though there is no public access to the shoreline. The steep valley sides have a number of well-maintained paths with occasional seats.

Time clearly wasn't of great importance to the Ravenfield estate workers in the 18th century, for the church clock only has an hour hand. St James was one of only three churches designed by famous Yorkshire architect, John Carr, who built Cannon Hall and much of the Wentworth Woodhouse estate.

S Cross the stile in front of the church, continue down the centre of the field to Arbour Lane and turn **left**. Enter Ravenfield Park and descend the steps by an information panel. The path levels along the length of the valley before descending steps and crossing a boardwalk. It continues through bracken and birch scrub, crosses Hooton Brook at the far end of the park and bears **right** alongside the boundary wall.

2 Where the path bends right, continue alongside the wall for 50m before veering away to ascend steeply through the wood. Turn **right** on a pleasant grassy path along the eastern boundary to eventually meet a track by a seat. Turn **right** with the ponds close by on your left. The track veers **right** at a gate and becomes a grassy footpath, which eventually meets the wall again at point **2**. Turn **left**, cross the bridge and follow your outward path back.

OPTIONAL ROUTE

The walk can be extended by turning **left** upon leaving the park. Hidden away at the bottom of Arbour Lane is the secluded and little known Firsby Reservoirs Local Nature Reserve, a small but delightful area of wetland wilderness. Enter the reserve and turn **right** along the track. As it swings left, go straight on along a natural path between trees. The path follows a convoluted course around the periphery of the reserve, only reaching open water near the end. Descend the steps beyond the house, rejoin Arbour Lane and thence back to Ravenfield.

7.25 km / 4.5 miles

16 Herringthorpe Valley & Brecks Plantation

We explore two well-maintained **Fuelling a Revolution**
woods within a park before heading east to investigate
the hidden valleys of Brecks Plantation.

7.25 km / 4.5 miles

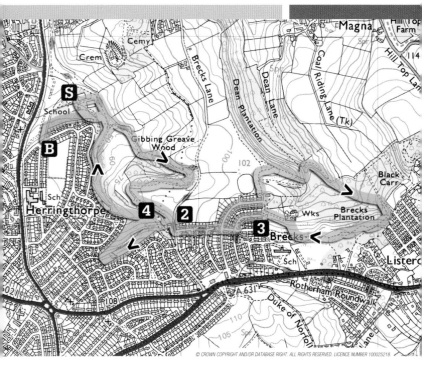

© CROWN COPYRIGHT AND/OR DATABASE RIGHT. ALL RIGHTS RESERVED. LICENCE NUMBER 100025218.

START Herringthorpe Valley Park on Brookside, off Herringthorpe Lane, signposted from the A6123 Herringthorpe Valley Road.

GRID REF SK 454926.

PARKING Herringthorpe Valley Park.

PUBLIC TRANSPORT

Bus service 14. *Train* from Sheffield and Barnsley. *There is an entrance to the park close to the bus stop opposite Woodall Road on Herringthorpe Lane. Leave the tarmac after 50 yards and follow the path right to the car park.*

TERRAIN A hilly walk with several climbs on a variety of surfaces.

REFRESHMENTS None.

OS MAP Explorer 278, Sheffield, Barnsley and Rotherham, South sheet.

16 Herringthorpe Valley & Brecks Plantation

Gibbing Greave and Herringthorpe Woods are both ancient replanted, primarily of beech. Their parkland situation, close proximity to Rotherham and the new multi-user Heritage Trail means access and footpath maintenance are to a high standard.

S Take the surfaced path from the bottom right-hand corner of the car park between the tennis and basketball courts and turn **right**. Beyond the children's playground, pass through the barrier and turn **left** on the Valley Park Heritage Trail. The tarmac ends at a Fuelling a Revolution information panel at the entrance to Gibbing Greave Wood. Descend the steps and cross the tiny bridge. Climb more steps into an open glade with a seat and continue. At the end of the wood, turn **right** across a plank footbridge and branch **right** along the edge of the slope. Bear **left** at a fork on the upper path that runs parallel with the woodland boundary and turn **left** at the end. *Just beyond this point it is worth a tiny detour through the gap on your right into the Valley Park to take in the view, looking over to Wentworth Woodhouse with its follies displayed across the horizon.* Take the footpath to the **left** of the Heritage Trail opposite the gap and ascend the steps. Leave the wood through a gap beyond a seat and cross a short field.

Brecks is private woodland in which a stone quarrying industry once thrived. It is well used by the local community and has a good network of unofficial paths. There are still private property signs at some entrances alongside the stiles and gates allowing you in. The area is characterised by several small streams that have carved steep and narrow wooded valleys, which are a joy to explore.

2 Turn **right** and then **left** into Belcourt Road. At the top, continue up the steps to the junction and turn **left**. At the end of the crescent, turn **left** between concrete posts and enter Brecks Plantation. You touch upon an open field with a vista to your left. Continue through the edge of the wood and turn **right** on the path clinging to the top of the steep slope. Descend gently into the valley and double back **left** between banks. Continue to descend and cross the wide plank footbridge to the **right**. Our path hugs the left bank, and higher up follows the **left** fork of the stream, which you stay alongside back into the wood to a prominent junction. Turn **right**

across the stream and follow the wide path uphill. Continue on the same line where it narrows (**right** fork) and turn **right** at a T-junction into a clearing. Branch **right** and continue a fair distance along the top of the slope until you round a fallen tree to a junction. A school wall topped with railings can be seen to your left. Bear **right** and descend into the open. The ornamental trees suggest this might once have been formal parkland.

3 Fork **left** to the exit and along the crescent. Turn **right** down Gibbing Greaves Road, continue down Belcourt Road to Brecks Lane and pass through the ornamental posts back into Herringthorpe Wood. Turn **left** at the seat to a hairpin bend below the Scout building and descend to a footbridge close to an information panel. Ascend the steps climbing Great Bank and turn **right**, continuing to ascend alongside garden fences. As you progress, glimpses of the view open up, and in May look out for the rare sight of white bluebells. Double back sharply **right** just before the housing estate and descend back to the footbridge spanning Herringthorpe Beck to complete the circuit of Great Bank.

On the left over the bridge are the remains of a piece of environmental art called the Crocodile and Clock. There isn't a great deal left of the croc, but you can count twelve tree stumps in a circle amidst the undergrowth.

4 Rejoin the Heritage Trail and turn **left** beside the stream. Continue past yet another information panel and keep **left** inside the trees. Beyond a stepped boardwalk, bear **right** with the stream and re-enter the Valley Park along a tarmac path. Pass through the barrier, turn **left** alongside a row of trees and **right** along the access road. For the bus, pass through the gap in the fence on your **left**, follow the path alongside the fence and turn **left**.

17 Wath Wood & Roman Ridge

Viking Longboat Bridge.

This remarkably rural walk is situated in a corridor of countryside between Rawmarsh and Swinton. It features two Fuelling a Revolution woods, two nature reserves, an ancient earthwork and the historic Waterloo Kiln, site of the famed Rockingham Pottery. The walk starts from Victoria Park – acquired by Rawmarsh council in 1901 – and formerly the grounds of Rosehill Victoria Hall.

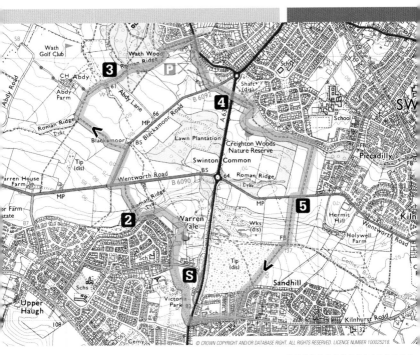

© CROWN COPYRIGHT AND/OR DATABASE RIGHT. ALL RIGHTS RESERVED. LICENCE NUMBER 100025218.

START Rosehill Victoria Park, Rawmarsh, signposted off the A633 along Old Warren Vale.

GRID REF SK 439973.

PARKING Rosehill Victoria Park.

PUBLIC TRANSPORT

Bus services 22, 108, 109 and 228. Services 22, 22X, and 22M from Barnsley. *Train* from Sheffield and Barnsley. Bus stops are outside the entrance to the park opposite Kilnhurst Road. *Enter Victoria Park and turn right, deviating off the tarmac and passing to the right of the bandstand to the car park.*

TERRAIN A mixture of improved and field paths. One prolonged ascent.

REFRESHMENTS None.

OS MAP Explorer 278, Sheffield, Barnsley and Rotherham, South sheet.

17 Wath Wood & Roman Ridge

The steep sides of Collier Beck are the clue to Birch Wood's status as ancient woodland. The "Monster of Birch Wood" footbridge was designed by Sheffield artist Jason Thomsom with the help of local schoolchildren. Made of steel in the shape of a Viking longboat, it has been left to rust and so blend with the environment.

Wath is a Fuelling a Revolution wood, which, like Birch Wood, is a remnant of common land, enclosed in the 18th century. The earthwork marked on OS maps as Roman Ridge was built at roughly the same time as the Iron Age fort in Scholes Coppice (Walk 20, p86), to defend the Celtic kingdom of Elmet from the Anglo Saxons.

S Continue beyond the car park and the sculptured tree and take the tarmac path **right** past the fenced beech tree to Wentworth Road. Take the path opposite, and after 150m turn **right** into the wood. The path winds down into Warren Vale Nature Reserve, formerly the site of Rawmarsh Colliery's Victoria Pit. The reserve, which includes Birch Wood, was designated in 1993. At a T-junction beneath overhead wires, turn **left** on a better-defined path that rises into open grassland. Turn **left** at the corner towards the houses and alongside them into Birch Wood to a sculptured footbridge by a Fuelling a Revolution seat.

2 Cross the bridge and ascend along the field edge. Turn **left** and then **right** into Blackamoor Road, which has a good grassy path along the verge. Turn **left** on the signed footpath and cross the stone stile at the corner. Turn **right** just past the electricity poles and **right** along the track. Where Abdy Lane bears right, enter Wath Wood at a stile.

3 Follow the path along the edge of the wood with the golf course on your left. Pass a waymarker post, cross a tarmac path to another post and continue ahead up the rise (path not waymarked). You are soon ascending the spine of the Roman Ridge, which is better defined higher up. Turn left at a waymark post and follow these steeply uphill. Note the exposed tree roots on your right and the earthwork going left. Turn **right** through

8 km / 5 miles

a barrier along an enclosed path to the A633. Turn **right** and, after 100m, **right** again along the signed footpath to Pottery Ponds. Pass through the metal gate and walk around the pond. Descend the steps and continue to the Waterloo Pottery Kiln, inside which is an information panel.

Retrace your steps, turn **right** and follow the fence to another information point. Bear **right** down the field to the exit. This grassy area is a pleasant picnic spot.

4 Take the path opposite and cross the A633 into Creighton Woods Nature Reserve. Within a few metres of joining a roughly surfaced path, leave it for a path going **right** at a fence corner and follow this around the perimeter of the wood. Turn **left** 10m before reaching a substantial plank footbridge over a shallow ditch then **right** after 20m. Pass through the green barrier and turn **right** beyond the end of the first field. Walk along the edge of the amenity grassland to the road.

5 Turn **right** and after 50m cross to a kissing gate opposite. There are good forward views from this path. Cross a boardwalk, turn **right** and ascend alongside an area of reclaimed land. Pass through an A-frame along a surfaced path and turn **right** along Kilnhurst Road to reach the A633. Enter Victoria Park and turn **right**, deviating off the tarmac and passing to the **right** of the bandstand to the car park.

The Swinton pottery was founded in 1745 by Joseph Flint. It later became the renowned Rockingham Pottery, noted for its fine porcelain, exhibits of which are housed in Clifton Park Museum. The kiln was built in 1815, the same year as the famous battle.

18 Grange Park Woodlands

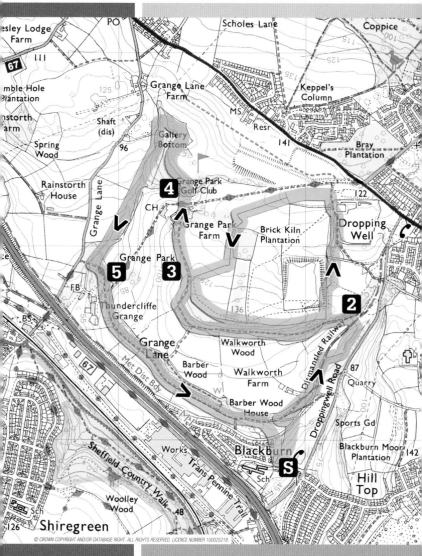

9 km / 5.5 miles

Keppel's Column from Grange Park.

Grange Park, the former estate of the Earl of Effingham, is home to a golf course, various sports facilities, no less than five Fuelling a Revolution woods and some of the finest meadowland in South Yorkshire. This meandering route showcases the best Grange Park has to offer – a summer walk not to be missed.

START Car park on Baring Road, opposite Blackburn Junior School.
GRID REF SK 388929.
PARKING Car park on Baring Road.
PUBLIC TRANSPORT
Bus service 7. *Train* from Sheffield and Barnsley to Meadowhall then the 43, or walk 1km along the Trans Pennine Trail to New Droppingwell Road.

TERRAIN A mixture of improved and natural paths through the woods, grassy trails outside. One short, but steep, stream crossing requiring care.
REFRESHMENTS Grange Park Golf Club. The bar is open to the public for refreshments and lunches.
T 01709 559497.
OS MAP Explorer 278, Sheffield, Barnsley and Rotherham, South sheet.

18 Grange Park Woodlands

Beyond the A-frame don't be startled by the crouching figure of a nude woman: It is only Yaiza, Carer of the Wild.

S Pass through the A-frame at the centre of the car park into the recreation area and continue past the shelter to a grassy footpath heading north through the gap between trees. Turn **left** along the track then **right** at the waymarked junction along a dismantled railway.

At a rock bearing the words "And gentle hermits singing" (as they do), descend **right** alongside the wall and turn **left** to a footbridge, where you meet Yaiza again, waiting patiently with her arms folded. Bear left up the slope to meet Yaiza yet again. She is now clearly embarrassed at you seeing her naked.

Walkworth supplied charcoal for smelting iron ore. Once it became part of the Effingham estate in the 18th century it was augmented with non-native trees and left unmanaged.

2 Cross over and ascend **left**, following the path into Walkworth Wood.

Continue past the steps and turn **right** at the junction by a seat to pass the Walkworth Wood information panel. Ascend to a seat with grand views over the golf course and M1 towards the vast sprawl of Greno Wood.

3 Follow the path **right** to the practice ground and turn **right** to a kissing gate. Ascend the meadow with trees on your right. Curve **left** alongside the upper fringe of Walkworth Wood, pass through a gate to a junction and go **straight on** along the edge of the field. Follow the path **left** into the next field and go **straight on** alongside the wooded bank, passing to the left of the football pitches. Cross the end of the tarmac and keep the same direction up the hill towards the fence, where you join an improved path. Turn **left** along the road for 50m then **left** between boulders into a delightful area of gorse and wild scrubland. Pass through a kissing gate and take the **right** fork. Continue through the gap, bear **left** and then **right** around the perimeter of the practice ground to the kissing gate at point **3**, thus completing the meadowland loop.

Don't veer left with the path, but go **straight on** with the practice ground on your right. Bear **right** at the tee alongside the wall and follow the track to the car park (clubhouse to your left).

These beautifully restored meadows are an absolute delight to walk in spring and summer. As the season progresses, new species and orchids appear. Until the late summer cut they are a haven for insects and butterflies.

Keppel's Column from Grange Park.

18 Grange Park Woodlands

Gallery Bottom can be traced back to the 13th century when it formed part of the medieval Kimberworth Deer Park. It was also subject to opencast mining for coal and iron ore. One of the surviving bell pits is visited shortly.

4 Pass the gap in the fence if you require refreshments at the clubhouse (or just lunch at the picnic tables round the back). Otherwise turn **right** to continue and cross the tee at the end of the paving stones to enter Gallery Bottom at a waymarker post.

Ascend past a seat into a clearing. Re-enter woodland and turn **left** at a waymarked junction. Bear **right** at the next post and keep to the **right** at the next junction for few metres before turning **left** on the path parallel with the stream. Pass an unwaymarked post, cross a tributary and continue by the stream to a seat. Turn **right** up to the tee and turn **left** along the edge of the fairway to reach a pond. Cross the bridge, follow the ditch to another pond and carry on through the trees to meet a track – turn **left**.

Originally the home of the Earls of Effingham until sold to John Baring in 1860, Thundercliffe Grange passed to Rotherham Borough Council in 1944. In June, the rhododendrons, foxgloves and flower meadows make Barber Wood, named after its 16th century owner, the most colourful of the woods on this walk. Woolley Wood, explored on Walk 3 (p12), lines the other side of the valley.

5 Turn right at the T-junction then turn **left** at the road, the access drive for Thundercliffe Grange. Bear **left** at the public footpath sign between stone pillars into Barber Wood, soon passing a quarry from which stone was taken for a rebuild in 1777.

After 1km, and 50m before reaching a green barrier, turn **right** beneath the arch of a fallen tree. Cross the field to a gate beside an electricity pole and go **straight on** past the playground to the car park.

Yaiza, Carer of the Wild.

19 Anston Stones & the Chesterfield Canal

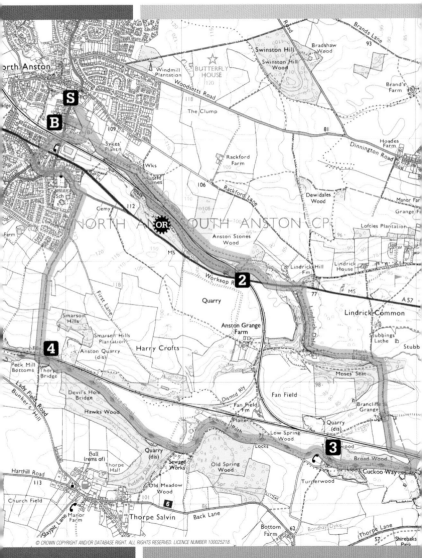

© CROWN COPYRIGHT AND/OR DATABASE RIGHT. ALL RIGHTS RESERVED. LICENCE NUMBER 100025218.

11.25 km / 7 miles

Anston Stones Wood.

We combine farmland, a rural canal and SSSI status meadowland and woodland on this exceptionally beautiful walk. A shorter circuit of 4km within the Anston Stones Wood Nature Reserve is included.

START Anston recreation ground, off the B6060, Ryton Road, opposite Anston Brook Primary School, North Anston.
GRID REF SK 522843.
PARKING Anston Parish Hall.
PUBLIC TRANSPORT
Bus service 19. On Sundays 19a or 19b to Dinnington Interchange then X5. Service X5 from Sheffield.
Train from Barnsley.

TERRAIN Improved towpath and paths in the nature reserve; the rest mostly dry. One long gradual ascent.
REFRESHMENTS Loyal Trooper, South Anston, near the end of the walk. Good Beer Guide pub serving lunchtime meals. *T* 01909 562203; Kiosk at Turnerwood.
OS MAP Explorer 279, Doncaster, South sheet.

19 Anston Stones & the Chesterfield Canal

The magnesian limestone gorge of Anston Stones, purchased from the Duke of Leeds in 1947, is both a Local Nature Reserve and a Site of Special Scientific Interest (SSSI). It is home to more woodland plant and grassland species than anywhere else in South Yorkshire. The meadows are nothing short of spectacular in late June and July when the orchids flower.

S Cross to the far right-hand corner of the recreation ground (from Ryton Road follow the track); pass through the kissing gate and immediately enter the field. Follow the narrow improved path and bear **left** at the junction, overlooking the river. Branch **left** along the upper path and follow the worn path along the edge of an area of grassland and into the wood at the far corner.

Descend the steps, but ignore the long flight going down into the wood. You soon enter the atmospheric gorge, which I've seen described as both 'Tolkein-esque' and reminiscent of the Brazilian rainforest. A little overdramatic, perhaps, but the pockmarked rock faces strewn with ivy, shallow caves, gnarled tree roots and dense canopy do lend a distinctive aura. You emerge for a while into flower meadows, a botanist's paradise in June and July when the grass is strewn with common spotted and pyramidal orchids and many rarities. As soon as the path re-enters the wood, branch **right** down the steps and cross Anston Brook, where there is an information panel.

OPTIONAL ROUTE

For a shorter circuit of 4km, turn **right**, pass under the railway and follow the river back to the start.

Lindrick golf course, founded in 1891, hosted the Ryder Cup in 1957 when the British famously beat the USA 7-4, the first victory since 1933. It took until 1985 to win it again outright. Other major championships hosted here include the Dunlop Masters, Curtis Cup, Ladies British Open and English Women's Amateur Championship in 2009. Greg Norman once took 14 strokes at the 17th in the 1982 Martini tournament.

2 Bear **left** and ascend to the A57. Turn **left** and cross the road. 100m along the grass verge, past the turning into Lindrick Dale, turn **right** at a public footpath sign and follow the yellow posts to the golf course. Walk down the edge of the fairway and behind the green, following the hedge into woodland, ignoring the A-frame on the right.

Heed the warning signs whilst crossing the fairways, turn **right** at a bridleway sign and cross the river. Bear **left** over a canal feeder and up through a strip of

11.25 km / 7 miles

woodland to a viewpoint. Continue to the farm, turn **left** along the lane and **right** at the end of the wall. Follow the improved path around the perimeter of the field, pass under the railway and continue to meet the canal at Cinderhill Lock. A few strides to your right you'll find an information panel.

3 At Turnerwood you can see the original information panel from 1982 and obtain refreshments from the kiosk (when open). The canal takes on a different aspect as you pass Old Spring and Hawks Wood lining the far bank. With no more locks, it more resembles a river, flowing between grassy banks.

4 Leave the canal at the Cuckoo Way signpost at bridge 32 and cross the railway. The path ascends arrow straight through fields to South Anston. Turn **left** along the lane and **left** again at the T-junction into the village. Pass St James' Church and go straight on down past the Loyal Trooper pub. Turn **right** just past the Methodist Church Community Hall along Chapel Walk and cross the A57 to the footpath beside the petrol station. Turn **left** under the bridge for the bus stops. For the car park, pass through the kissing gate, cross the stream and branch **left** at Turner's Field interpretive board.

Engineered by James Brindley, the Chesterfield Canal was begun in 1771 and became operational in 1777. It transported mainly coal, but more famously the stone used to build the current Houses of Parliament. From the terminus at West Stockwith the locally-quarried stone was transported by sloop along the Trent and Humber to the North Sea, then up the Thames to Westminster. It took three years. The collapse of the Norwood Tunnel in 1907 split the canal in two. Traffic ceased altogether in 1962. Right up to the end, all cargoes were horse drawn.

The 46-mile towpath from Chesterfield to West Stockwith is designated the Cuckoo Way (the boats were known as cuckoos). This 4km stretch is scenically the best of the whole route, though you will be extremely lucky to see a canal boat here! Being a dead end and containing a huge number of locks, only the very dedicated get this far.

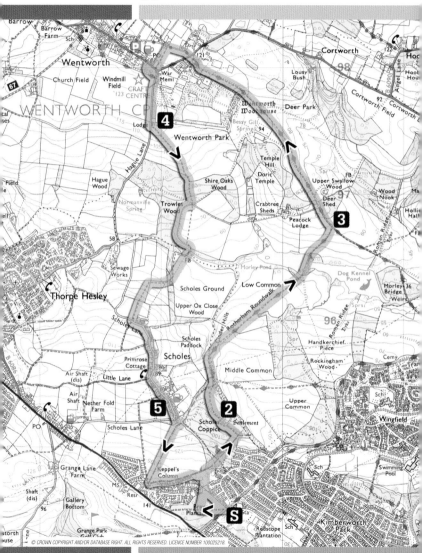

11.25 km / 7 miles

Wentworth Woodhouse. PHOTO: David Coefield

A walk through history, beginning with an Iron Age earthwork hidden inside a Fuelling a Revolution wood, followed by Wentworth Woodhouse, built on the wealth of the coal industry, and finishing with the magnificent viewpoint of Keppel's Column, seen from a distance on many of the walks in this book.

START Public footpath sign pointing into Bray Plantation on Oaks Lane opposite Barkers Park.

GRID REF SK 396945.

PARKING Side road off Oaks Lane just past Barkers Park.

PUBLIC TRANSPORT
Bus services 39, 40 and 43. Service 66 from Sheffield stops at the junction of Oaks Lane and the A629. *Train* from Barnsley to Meadowhall then the 43.

TERRAIN One prolonged ascent. Stout footwear recommended.

REFRESHMENTS The Rockingham Arms, Wentworth, *T* 01226 742075; and Wentworth Garden Centre Tea Room, *T* 01226 744842. Both at about halfway point.

OS MAP Explorer 278, Sheffield, Barnsley and Rotherham, South sheet.

20 Scholes Coppice & Wentworth Woodhouse

As the name suggests, Bray Plantation isn't ancient woodland. It was named after Jonathan Bray, who planted trees in the 1820s to hide the spoil left by the mining of ironstone and coal from shallow 'bell pit' excavations. The prolific overgrown humps are all around you.

There are two circular long distance walks around the borough of Rotherham. The Round Walk is 25 miles and marked on OS maps. The Ring Route, devised by the Ramblers Association Rotherham Metro Group, is 50 miles. The green bell motif recalls the bell manufacturing industry, which thrived in Rotherham for 200 years from 1615.

S Enter Bray Plantation at the footpath sign, head through the centre of the wood for 200m and turn **right** at a seat.

Pass a playground and ascend the steps into amenity grassland. Follow the Rotherham Ring Route **left** to reach Keppel's Field.

Turn **right** into Scholes Coppice, keep **right** straight on down the hill and turn **left** at the waymarker post at a cross-path. Straight in front of you at the next junction is a Fuelling a Revolution information panel relating the history of Scholes Coppice and Caesar's Camp. Though mostly hidden, the rampart is visible.

2 Rejoin the waymarked route and follow the path to the northernmost corner. Turn **right** on a concrete path, over a swamp and then **left** to leave the wood. Bear **right** beside the stream, following the Rotherham Round Walk.

Cross the stream and ascend into farmland. *From the top of the rise you have an initial view of all the main features of this walk. Behind you is Keppel's Column, to your left the spire of Wentworth church, then Wentworth Woodhouse, a folly, Hoober Stand and the Mausoleum.*

Continue over fields for 1km to Dog Kennel Pond, a silly name for what is probably the biggest lake in the book. The track bisects the lake to reach a junction with a tarmac lane.

Wentworth Church. PHOTO: David Coefield

20 Scholes Coppice & Wentworth Woodhouse

Wentworth Woodhouse is the largest stately home in the country, about twice the size of Buckingham Palace. The east front is 606ft long. Begun in 1734, the huge façade hides an older house to the rear. Taking the servants into account, 150 bedrooms weren't enough, so the Fitzwilliam's added another storey in 1782. Though a grade 1 listed building, the house has only recently been open to the public.

The mausoleum was commissioned in 1783 by the 4th Earl in memory of his uncle, the Marquis of Rockingham. Designed by John Carr and completed in 1788, it stands 90ft high and has three storeys, topped by a cupola. The enclosed ground floor contains a statue of the Marquis along with busts of his eight best friends. The open colonnade above contains an empty sarcophagus (Rockingham is buried in York Minster).

Designed by Henry Flitcroft, Hoober Stand was finished in 1748 to commemorate the overthrow of the Jacobite rebellion of 1745. It is a three-sided pyramid 100ft high, topped with a hexagonal lantern. The viewing platform is reached by an internal spiral staircase of 155 steps. Both are open on Sunday afternoons 2 – 5pm from Spring Bank Holiday to August Bank Holiday. The folly to your left is not open to the public.

3 Turn **left** and walk along the grass verge into Wentworth Park, formally the estate of the Earls Fitzwilliam until the line died out in 1979. Cross the cattle grid and stay with the road until a footpath sign points off to the **right**. Follow this to another metalled road passing to the **right** of the mansion.

You are soon able to walk on the grass again past the stables, built in 1768 by John Carr. It is sad to see the bell tower, sundial and clock in this state of neglect. Stay with the drive to reach the B6060 outside Wentworth village. Cross over into Clayfield Lane and pass the Round House, formerly a windmill, to a footpath sign on the **left**. Descend to the road and turn **right** towards the Rockingham Arms. If not calling in, cross the road at the post office into woodland and follow the path **left** to Hague Lane. Turn **right** and pass Wentworth Garden Centre, where there is a tea room and lots more besides. Where the footway ends, enter the lodge gates and cross the stile.

4 The path heads diagonally **left** down through the field to woodland (though outside of summer a line may not be visible.) *Note another folly to your left.* Follow the woodland edge to a stile in the corner. Continue on a grassy path, over a track to a stile and turn **right**, descending around the periphery of Trowles Wood to reach Morley Pond. Cross the bridge and cut the corner, following the waymarked path into the wood, past a ruined building and out the other side. Follow the fence to a stile and turn **left** uphill to one on the horizon. Continue by the hedge to Scholes Lane and turn **left** into the village.

5 Pass the Bay Horse (not open at lunchtimes during the week) and enter Scholes Coppice at a footpath sign on the bend where Scholes Village becomes Scholes Lane. Cross the stream and turn immediately **right** out of the wood into Keppel's Field. Ascend straight up through this local nature reserve to Keppel's Column, by which there is an information point.

Head **left** along the upper path with the housing estate on your right, noting the excellent view across all the countryside you have traversed today. Follow the fence beyond a stile to a gate with the Ring Route waymark. Cross the woodland and turn **right**, following the waymarkers past the playground and back into Bray Plantation. Take the first path on the **left** and skirt the edge of the wood back to Oaks Lane.

At 115ft, the Keppel's column is the highest of the Wentworth follies. It is dedicated to Admiral Keppel, a friend of the Marquis of Rockingham, who was court-martialled for failing to engage the French fleet during the Battle of Ushant, but later acquitted. The folly stood inside Scholes Coppice until the Second World War, when opencast mining decimated half the wood.

The Mausoleum, Wentworth Park.

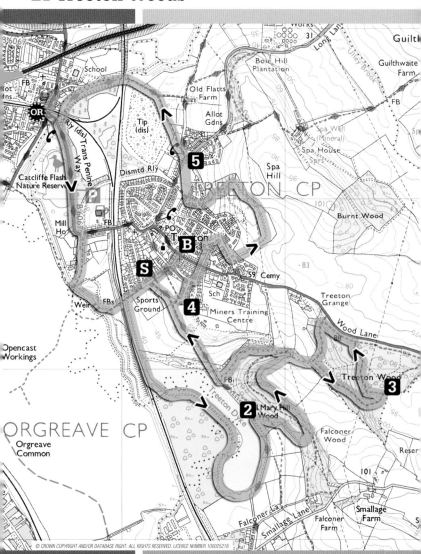

© CROWN COPYRIGHT AND/OR DATABASE RIGHT. ALL RIGHTS RESERVED. LICENCE NUMBER 100025218.

This varied walk is the epitome of what this guide is all about, using a number of footpaths not marked on the map to explore three attractive *Fuelling a Revolution* woods, areas of wetland, reclaimed colliery land and two lakes important for water birds. Its figure-of-eight layout means it can be split into two. The first loop features Treeton Dyke and the woods; the second Catcliffe Flash, a stretch of the River Rother and the historic Catcliffe Glass Cone.

START On Washfield Lane, outside Treeton Sports Ground.
GRID REF SK 432874.
PARKING Washfield Lane.
PUBLIC TRANSPORT
Bus service 72a and 73 (not Sundays) from Rotherham. Services 72a and 74 from Sheffield. *Train* from Barnsley.

TERRAIN Mostly natural paths and with several short climbs. Stout footwear recommended.
REFRESHMENTS Treeton Cricket clubhouse open to non-members at weekends. *T* 0114 269 2135.
OS MAP Explorer 278, Sheffield, Barnsley and Rotherham, South sheet.

21 Treeton Woods

Treeton Dyke is an artificial lake created by diverting the River Rother during construction of the railway, after which it served as a source of water for Orgreave Colliery.

S Walk to the bottom of Washfield Lane into the cul de sac, Hemmingway Close, and turn **left** on the track alongside the railway fence. Keep ahead upon reaching Treeton Dyke with the water on your left. Abandon the hard track beyond the green barrier for the grassy path branching **left**. Stay on the grass all the way along the lakeshore until eventually rejoining the hard track where it narrows to a footpath. Cross a fence and take the **left** fork around the head of the lake. Pass through a wooden barrier and turn **left**.

Falconer Wood (there is also a Falconer Lane and Falconer Farm) is named after Robert Faulkener, the landowner in 1311. Hail Mary Hill clearly has a religious connection and dates from when the area belonged to Nostell Priory. Treeton Wood was formerly called Oaken Cliff because it was an oak wood on a steep slope.

2 Enter Falconer Wood through an A-frame and, after 50m, turn **right** up a wide path. Bear **right** at a post along the woodland fringe then **left** at the fork waymarked *Doorstep Walk* to ascend through the wood. Continue with the Doorstep Walk over a path junction to reach the top of what is now Hail Mary Hill Wood. Emerge after a while into a small open space, continue down steps and branch **right** after 50m. At the bottom, turn **right** out of the wood and cross the field to enter Treeton Wood. Pass a seat and branch **right**. This path has a yellow arrow waymarker and follows the edge of the wood. Bear **left** at an unmarked fork and ascend, at first still close to the edge, before diverging and climbing with greater purpose.

3 At a junction of paths at the top, take the first on the **left**, pass through a clearing beneath power lines and continue on the waymarked path. This eventually runs parallel with Treeton Lane, which lies over the wall on your right. At the next post you will see an exit up to your right. Turn **left** downhill and **left** again past a post. At the next post, branch **right** along the edge of the wood and **right** again to leave the way you came in.

Catcliffe Glass Cone.

21 Treeton Woods

This area was once more open with large pools, but as reeds and waterside vegetation colonised the wetlands, trapping silt from the stream, the pools have become isolated, smaller and dryer, allowing willow to grow and form carr woodland, which, if allowed to dry out completely, would become birch scrub and then oak wood.

Re-enter Hail Mary Hill Wood and follow the low path by the stream. Fork **left** immediately beyond the steps, following the Doorstep Walk waymarker. Ignore a wide path going left and continue until Treeton Dyke looms through the trees. Turn **right** across the causeway over Treeton Marsh.

Cross the track and continue along the Trans Pennine Trail, which squeezes between boulders and heads back to Treeton. Squeeze through more boulders and bear **left**. There are improving views over the Dyke and the reclaimed land beyond. Fork **left** following the overhead wire, through two metal barriers to Washfield Lane to complete the first loop.

4 If you intend doing the whole walk today, turn **right** at the footpath sign in front of the first barrier and enter the cul de sac. Turn **right** at the junction and then **left** after 20m. Cross the zebra crossing, descend Pit Lane and pass through a gap beyond the Community Centre. Turn **right** and **right** again at the roundabout along High Hazel Road. Turn **left** into Windle Court, through the A-frame and ascend beneath power lines, following the path **left** around the perimeter of reclaimed land. There is an expansive view from the summit seat. *Can you pick out the conical shape of Catcliffe Glass Cone in front of the Parkway and Keppel's Column on the horizon?* Descend into Treeton alongside the fence. Fork **right**, cross Chandler Grove and take the next **right** through an A-frame into a recreation area.

5 Cross diagonally to the road by the playground and take the grassy footpath opposite, heading away from the row of terraced houses. Follow the small stream past an area of wetland to reach the River Rother, hidden behind its flood embankment. Despite this and other measures the Rother has the ungentlemanly habit of regularly flooding poor old Catcliffe, most notably in June 2007. Pass the picnic tables and under the railway, following the river along a surfaced path lined with wooden posts engraved with wildlife carvings.

OPTIONAL ROUTE

The top of Catcliffe Glass Cone comes into view just before the next bridge. It is but a short diversion **right** along Treeton Lane and again at the mini-roundabout. It is the oldest and most complete of only three surviving glass cones in the country. There is an information panel at the rear of the edifice.

Back on the route, cross Treeton Lane and turn **left** following the path separated from the road by a hedge.

Cross to the pavement opposite and continue along Treeton Lane. Cross the road just beyond the safety railings, pass through the kissing gate and green barrier. This raised wooded path is clearly a former railway line. Bear **left** alongside a fence and continue along the improved path, past a Waverley map board, through the kissing gate and over the railway bridge back into Washfield Lane.

Catcliffe Flash Nature Reserve is a recent feature formed as a result of mining subsidence. It is one in a string of three lakes lining the Rother Valley that is home to a large and varied population of winter breeding and visiting water birds. The layby attracts many a twitcher.

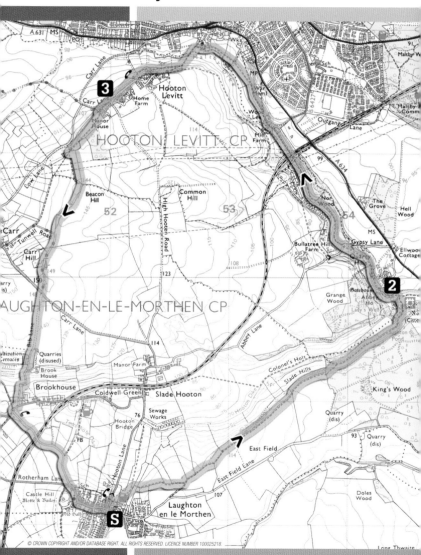

© CROWN COPYRIGHT AND/OR DATABASE RIGHT. ALL RIGHTS RESERVED. LICENCE NUMBER 100025218.

The focus of this walk is the Cistercian Roche Abbey, owned by English Heritage, but the endless panoramas of the surrounding area will probably be your most abiding memories, so try and pick a clear day to make the most of it.

START The junction of High Street and Hooton Lane, Laughton-en-le-Morthen.

GRID REF SK 520881.

PARKING By the bus stops on School Road close to the junction with High Street.

PUBLIC TRANSPORT
Bus services 19 and 19A. From Sheffield service X5 to Dinnington then 19 or 19A. *Train* from Sheffield and Barnsley.

TERRAIN Stout footwear recommended.

REFRESHMENTS Refreshments and toilets available at Roche Abbey when open.

OS MAP Explorer 279, Doncaster, South sheet.

22 Roche Abbey

Though now a small village in the middle of nowhere, you can see from the size of the tower and spire of All Saints Church that Laughton was once a prominent place. The village may have been founded near a battlefield as en-le-morthen is Old French for place of death. The locals liked to call it Lighten in the Morning, and who can blame them? The St Leger Arms is named after local MP Lt. Col. Anthony St Leger, a racehorse breeder from nearby Firbeck. The two-mile race he established at Doncaster for three year olds is now one of the great English classics.

Beautifully set in a valley landscaped by 'Capability' Brown in the 18th century, the most striking feature of this Cistercian abbey is the eastern end of its church, built in the new Gothic style c.1170. It has one of the most complete ground plans of any English Cistercian monastery, laid out as excavated foundations. It fell victim to the Dissolution in the sixteenth century. For a detailed history visit: www.cistercians.shef.ac.uk Visit www.english-heritage.org.uk and enter Roche Abbey for opening times and prices.

S Take Hooton Lane from the junction with High Street and turn **right** after 100m at the footpath sign. Walk around the edge of the field and descend 200m to a stile in the hedge. Pass through a gap and continue with the hedge on your left before switching back to reach a junction. Turn **left**, but before entering the field branch **right** into the trees. Continue along the edge of the field on a gradual ascent. The path levels out along a splendid promenade offering fine views at first to the left and later straight ahead. Ignore a track dipping left and pass a viewpoint seat. Enter King's Wood, descend **left** and turn **right** at the junction. Cross the stepping stones. You pass a picturesque lake and then Roche Abbey comes into view over to the right. Continue along the track to reach the ruins of the gatehouse.

2 A footpath encircles the site and I would strongly recommend you walk this, as it provides excellent close-up views of the ruins. Re-cross the stepping stones, repeat your inward route to the gatehouse and turn **left** along the track, which becomes a footpath beyond the car park. Cross the road into the wooded valley of Maltby Dike. After a long stretch by the stream, the path climbs gently to a prominent fork; bear **right** uphill. Bear **left** at the junction and immediately **left** again to pass beneath the railway. Descend into the open with a fence on your left.

Cross the road and continue alongside the hedge into amenity grassland with St Bartholomew's church ahead. Take either the barely distinguishable path across the middle of the field or the main path to the top corner and turn **left** down the surfaced path. Both lead to a kissing gate in the hedge, beyond which aim for the church spire. Cross Maltby Dike at a footbridge beyond the church and ascend a flight of steps. Just inside the wood branch **right** at the footpath sign along the lower fringe. Bear **left** into Hooton Levitt and continue along the road with a low wall on your right.

3 Cross the road above the hairpin bend to a footpath sign on the right of Manor Farm Court. Continue beyond the development along the edge of the slope with excellent views. Beyond a waymarker post in a gateway, follow the hedge on your **left** up to a stile and continue with a wide vista to join the track called Tunwell Lane. This passes a transmitter mast to reach Carr Lane, where there is seat just to the right. Cross over and continue along Bib Lane to a junction. Turn **right** then **left** after 50m along Brookhouse Lane. This equally quiet byway ascends over a railway to Laughton. Enter the village and follow the road past the church to the start.

Keep your eyes open on the stretch between the transmitter and the road for what must be the most redundant OS column in Britain, standing forlorn and forgotten in the middle of the hedge on your left. At the dizzying height of 150m above sea level and on flat ground, it seems completely out of place, but the view from the seat is awesome. As The Who sang, you can see for miles and miles. With the vast skyscape and open arable fields you could be forgiven for thinking you're in East Anglia.

Barnsley

What the Barnsley area lacks in ancient woodland, it more than makes up for with its wealth of countryside visitor attractions, including Yorkshire Sculpture Park, Elsecar Heritage Centre, Cannon Hall Museum, Monk Bretton Priory, Wentworth Castle Gardens, Stainborough Park and Worsbrough Mill. Water also features strongly in these walks, with visits to Wombwell Ings, Gypsy Marsh Nature Reserve, the Dearne Valley Park, the wild Upper Don Valley and the Wetlands Centre at Old Moor RSPB Reserve – a birdwatcher's paradise.

Yorkshire Sculpture Park with Henry Moore's Two Piece Reclining Figure: Cut 1979-81. PHOTO: YSP/Jonty Wilde

Wentworth Castle. PHOTO: David Coefield

23 Old Moor RSPB Reserve

PHOTO: David Coefield

I recommend that this short walk beside a public lake and alongside the River Dearne be extended by visiting the reserve (free for members). It can be combined with walk 27, Wombwell Ings and Gypsy Marsh (p122). The reserve and this walk are well-suited to a winter visit, whereas walk 27 is much better underfoot in summer. Binoculars would enhance your enjoyment of this walk.

4.5 km / 2.8 miles

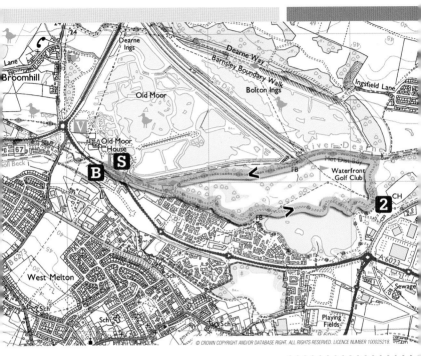

START RSPB Old Moor on the A633.
GRID REF SE 423022.
PARKING RSPB Old Moor.
PUBLIC TRANSPORT
Bus service 222 and X20 (not Sundays).
Train from Sheffield, Meadowhall and Rotherham.

TERRAIN Level walk on improved paths.
REFRESHMENTS Café at the Visitor Centre.
OS MAP Explorer 278, Sheffield, Barnsley and Rotherham, North sheet.

23 Old Moor RSPB Reserve

Old Moor Wetlands Reserve comprises 250 acres of open water, fenland, reedbed and marsh. The pools were formed through mining subsidence and from the removal of topsoil used to regenerate colliery spoil heaps. It is managed by the Royal Society for the Protection of Birds (RSPB). The Visitor Centre has toilets, a café and shop. Once inside follow the path to the right for the main hides. The path to the left features the short Wildlife Ponds Walk and a longer trek to just one hide.

S From the car park, cross the footbridge over Knoll Beck and turn **left** along the Trans Pennine Trail. Branch **right** at a fenced pond and, at a three-way fork, take the middle path passing to the left of an overgrown pond. Cross a footbridge and, after several hundred metres, reach open water. In dry conditions you can forsake the track for a while and walk along the grassy shore, rejoining the track where the lake bends to the right.

2 Bear **left** at a fork and pass beneath overhead wires. Follow the stream on your right a short distance and continue over the golf course to meet the River Dearne. Turn **left** along the Trans Pennine Trail for 2km back to the car park.

24 Cannon Hall

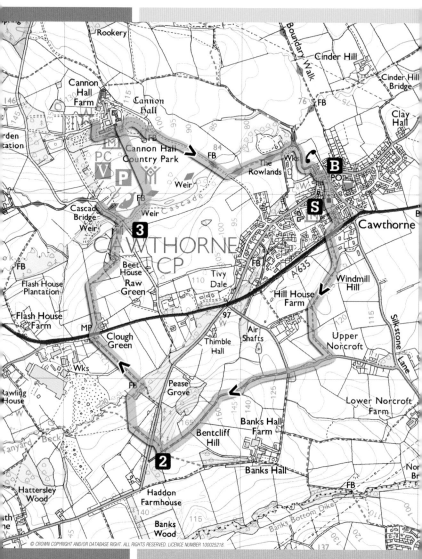

6.5 km / 4 miles

Cannon Hall.

We start from the attractive village of Cawthorne, visiting the Cannon Hall museum en route. There are, in fact, refreshments and museums in both Cawthorne and Cannon Hall if you pick the right day.

START All Saints Church, Cawthorne.
GRID REF SE 285080.
PARKING The Parish Hall behind the church. It is on Church Lane, off Church Street, between the Spencer Arms and gift shop. If full, park with consideration higher up Church Street.
PUBLIC TRANSPORT
Bus services Hourly service 92. *Train* from Sheffield, Meadowhall and Rotherham.

TERRAIN Mainly field and woodland paths. Stout footwear recommended.
REFRESHMENTS It could end up a bun-fest. There's the Thyme Bistro in Cannon Hall Garden Centre, Cannon Hall Farm Tea Room, The Spencer Arms and Cawthorne Antiques Tea Room (closed Wednesdays).
OS MAP Explorer 278, Sheffield, Barnsley and Rotherham, North sheet.

24 Cannon Hall

The museum is currently open April – October, Tuesday to Friday, 10am – 4pm, Weekends 11am – 4pm. Closed Mondays except Bank Holidays. Winter opening 12 – 4pm weekends from November to 24 December and February half-term to 31 March. Many of the rooms are preserved from when the hall was home to the Spencer-Stanhope family, who made their fortune from iron. Admission is free.

If you are ready for refreshment or fancy a browse, turn left along the road a short distance to Cannon Hall Garden Centre, which houses the Thyme Bistro. Alternatively, there is the farm teashop behind Cannon Hall car park. Both have toilets.

S From the parish hall, follow the path alongside the fence signposted *Norcroft Lane*. Cross the A635 and climb to the seat on Windmill Hill. Cross the stile, turn **right**, enter the next field and bear **left**. There is no discernible line, but head for the corner of the trees, then continue along the field edge to Norcroft Lane and turn **right**. At the bend, go straight on along the bridlepath between trees.

2 With the road in sight 50m away, turn **right** at a waymarker post. Cross the road and continue along the field edge. Cross two stiles, bear **right** and head diagonally down across the field. A stile soon comes into view. Go straight on at the waymarker post down steps, cross a footbridge and ascend past a redundant stile into fields. Cross the A635 to a stile by the old milepost. After 50m cross the stile in the wall on the **left** and continue alongside the hedge with Cannon Hall in the foreground. Pass through a gap in the hedge with a circular water trough just beyond. Bear **right** to the yellow painted stile to the right of the mobile phone mast. Follow the fence to a stile beyond a cattle grid and continue down the field.

3 Cross the road to the kissing gate and enter Cannon Hall Country Park. Walk beside the lake, cross the footbridge below the weir and continue straight up across the park to the hall. Aim for the footbridge to the right of the house and continue to The Pinery, once a hothouse for growing exotic plants. Pass through the Walled Garden and out **left** through the Cottage Garden, both of which have information panels. Walk around the front of the hall to the museum entrance on the other side.

6.5 km / 4 miles

Retrace your steps round the front of the hall, continue past The Pinery and bear **left** on a cinder path through rhododendron and ornamental woodland. Pass through the stone arch and descend alongside the hedge. Cross the Palladian Bridge and branch **left** to join the fence on your right. Pass the cricket ground and continue alongside the wall. Cross the clapper bridge and follow the improved path into Cawthorne. Turn **left** and then **right** into Church Street and bear **right** at the drinking fountain to All Saints Church, passing the grassy track to the museum. Pass to the **right** of the church to the parish hall.

Behind the hall is Cannon Hall Farm, a visitor attraction for families. There is a farm shop, a café and toilets. There is an admission charge to the farm and adventure playground.

Cawthorne Museum is open Saturdays, Sundays and Bank Holiday Mondays from 2 – 5pm from Palm Sunday to the end of October. Founded in 1884 by the Rev. Charles Tiplady Pratt, it houses an interesting collection of Victorian memorabilia. There is a nominal charge.

Cannon Hall gardens.

25 Dearne Valley Park & Monk Bretton Priory

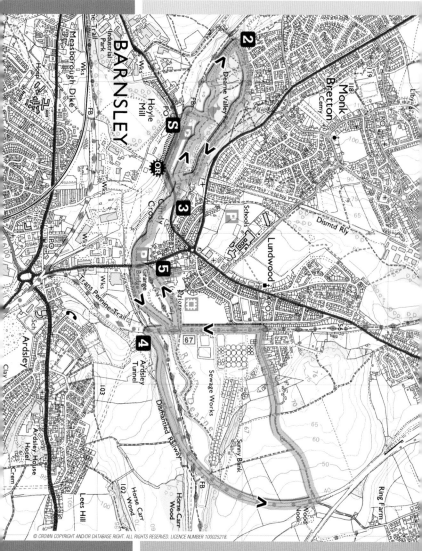

© CROWN COPYRIGHT AND/OR DATABASE RIGHT. ALL RIGHTS RESERVED. LICENCE NUMBER 100025218.

9.75 km / 6 miles

The substantial remains of Monk Bretton Priory border Dearne Valley Park, which lies just a mile from Barnsley town centre. Developed in 1980, it became a Local Nature Reserve in 1996. We walk beside lakes, the defunct Barnsley Canal and the River Dearne, and then loop back along two branches of the Trans Pennine Trail to visit the priory.

START Dearne Valley Country Park on the A628 Pontefract Road, opposite The Spice of India restaurant.
GRID REF SE 364066.
PARKING Dearne Valley Country Park.
PUBLIC TRANSPORT
Bus services 27, 30 and 32. *Train* from

Sheffield, Meadowhall and Rotherham.
TERRAIN A variety of surfaces, all good underfoot in dry conditions.
REFRESHMENTS None.
OS MAP Explorer 278, Sheffield, Barnsley and Rotherham, North sheet.

25 Dearne Valley Park & Monk Bretton Priory

The stone support pillars are all that remain of the five-arched aqueduct that once spanned the Dearne Valley. The canal was built at the turn of the 19th century to transport coal from the Barnsley pits the sixteen miles to the River Calder. Mining subsidence made it costly to maintain, and leakage from the aqueduct forced its closure in 1945, after which most of it was filled in.

S With the main road on your left, pass a circular mosaic and information panel and cross the footbridge over the River Dearne. Bear **right**, cross a smaller footbridge and turn **left** at the tip of the lake. You have a view over the water to Oakwell, the home of Barnsley Football Club. Continue alongside a second, much narrower, lake, gradually gaining height. At the summit, make a short diversion down some steps to the **left** and cross the bridge (the site of the former aqueduct of the Barnsley Canal). Climb the steps to view the only section still holding water.

2 Retrace your steps and continue along the broad grassy swathe of the defunct canal. Beyond the houses you pass Cliffe Wood, one of only three Fuelling a Revolution woods in the Barnsley area. Further on, the winding gear of the preserved pithead of Barnsley Main Colliery is visible across the valley. Reaching a stone buttress, cross a path and descend a flight of steps. Continue out of the wood to a junction and turn **left** at the waymark post.

3 Cross Pontefract Road and re-enter the park. At the path junction, go straight on, but leave the tarmac after 30m to join the riverbank. Bear **left** downstream to Grange Lane, cross over and rejoin the river. Bear **left** at the bridge, ascend the tarmac path and double back **right** along the Trans Pennine Trail.

4 Turn **left** at the junction along the old Midland Railway, where there is a choice of surfaces. Cross Sunny Bank viaduct and turn **left** over fields to Lundwood. Continue beyond the barrier down Lund Lane and turn **left** along the Trans Pennine Trail. Branch **right** back down into Dearne Valley Park and stay with the tarmac.

5 Turn **right** at the junction and pass through the archway along Abbey Lane to the entrance of Monk Bretton Priory.

Return to the park and turn **right** to Grange Lane. Retrace your steps along the riverbank or follow the tarmac to Pontefract Road. (I would advise crossing at the far exit, as visibility at the outward crossing point is limited in this direction.)

OPTIONAL ROUTE

There is a shortcut back to the car park by crossing the river and turning **right** along the tarmac path.

For the main route, turn **right** and retrace your steps to the junction. Turn **right** at the waymark post and then **left** at the bottom of the steps into the wood. Bear **left** at a fork down steps to join the river. Upon reaching the lake, turn **left** to the car park.

Founded in 1154 by Adam Fitz Swain, the Priory was staffed by French monks based at St John's Clunaic Priory in Pontefract, before becoming an independent Benedictine monastery in 1281. 60 years after the Dissolution, the Earl of Shrewsbury bought the remains as a wedding gift for his fourth son, Henry Talbot. Barnsley council manage the site in conjunction with English Heritage. It is open daily from 10:30am – 3pm and admission is free. Interpretive panels are scattered across the site. The stone-lined drainage system is particularly impressive.

The Mill of the Black Monks was built in the 11th century and claims to be the oldest in England. It started life as the water mill for the priory and has – as you would expect with such a name – been investigated for paranormal activity.

The Gatehouse, Monk Bretton Priory. PHOTO: David Coefield

26 Elsecar Heritage Centre

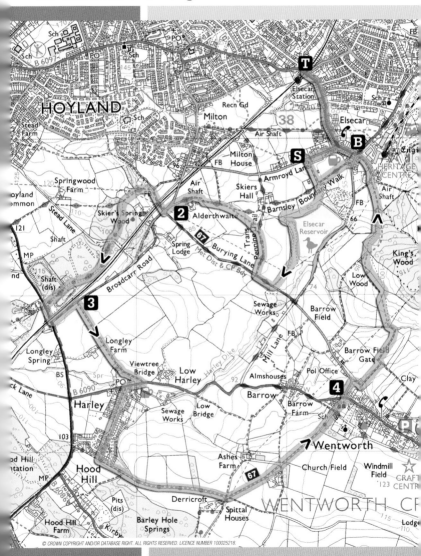

We visit Elsecar Heritage Centre at the end of this varied walk through fields, woods and by a lake. The workshops now house craft shops, exhibitions, a café and toilets. Special events are staged throughout the year. To plan your walk to coincide with something that takes your fancy, like a ride on a steam train or to see the Newcomen Beam Engine, check the 'Your Visit' and 'What's On' pages at **www.elsecar-heritage.com**

START Elsecar Park on Armroyd Lane.
GRID REF SK 382998.
PARKING Elsecar Park.
PUBLIC TRANSPORT
Bus service 66. Service 227 from Rotherham. *Train* from Barnsley, Sheffield and Meadowhall to Elsecar on the Nottingham to Leeds service. From Rotherham, change to this service at Meadowhall. *Turn right out of the station down Hill Street and right on Armroyd Lane (10 mins).*
TERRAIN A mixture of surfaces.

REFRESHMENTS Café in Elsecar Park is open seven days a week, closing at 4pm (5pm at weekends) April to October. It closes an hour earlier in winter. Café in Elsecar Heritage Centre open every day. The Horseshoe at Harley, about halfway round (not open at lunchtime during the week) *T* 01226 742204 and The Market in Elsecar at the end of the walk *T* 01266 740240. Both Good Beer Guide pubs.
OS MAP Explorer 278, Sheffield, Barnsley and Rotherham, South sheet.

26 Elsecar Heritage Centre

PHOTO: David Coefield

S Follow the signed lane at the western end of the car park into Elsecar Park. Pass between the playground and café and turn **right** along the Timberland Trail, which doubles as our old friend the Trans Pennine Trail. Pass through the barrier and continue alongside the reservoir, constructed in 1794 to provide water for the Barnsley Canal. It is now a Local Nature Reserve. At the signpost, turn **left** over the bridge on the alternative route for walkers only. Keep straight on at a fork and pass beneath overhead wires to a road.

Turn **right** and **right** again on the Trans Pennine Trail East. Turn **left** at the point where the hedge meets taller trees, emerge into open fields and progress along a line of occasional trees, some of which are fenced in. Join the field boundary and head for the farm. A stile leads into a narrow plantation. Descend the steps and turn **left** alongside the hedge. Beyond the ruinous farm buildings pass through the gateway and turn **right** along the drive.

2 Cross the road and turn **right** at the junction. Go straight on through a metal gate to a stile on the left after 75m. Turn **left** beyond the next stile and ascend the steps to enter Skier's Spring Wood. Bear **left** down to Stead Lane, kink **right** and **left** along a tarmac track. This crosses reclaimed land to meet the A6135 through the yard of a garage. Turn **left** and **left** again into Broadcarr Road. Walk along the right-hand verge to a gap on the **right** just before the end of the brick wall on the other side of the road.

3 Follow the fence on your **left** and the stream beyond the houses to the road. Turn **right** to The Horseshoe and **left** along Occupation Road. At the junction beyond the cricket ground, go straight on along the path between

9.75 km / 6 miles

houses and turn **left**. Turn **right** into Coach Road, which should be free of traffic, and eventually turn **left** at the junction along the Trans Pennine Trail to Wentworth.

4 Cross the main road into Barrowfield Lane and turn **right** at the bend. Follow the farm track round to the **left**. It runs between hedges to a signed junction; turn **left** and then **right**. Emerge from between hedges and cross the field. Bear **right** along the nearside of the hedge, pass through a gap and turn **left**. Towards the bottom of the field the path curves away from the hedge to enter King's Wood. Fork **left** along the woodland fringe, cross the field and go straight on through a metal barrier to Elsecar Heritage Centre. The entrance is opposite the Market Hotel.

Leave the way you came in and either walk up Fitzwilliam Street to the station or turn **left** for 50m along Wentworth Road to the footpath sign. An enclosed path emerges in the park by the café. Turn **right** back along the lane to the car park.

Wentworth has two Holy Trinity churches, the partly ruinous medieval old church, which is maintained by the Churches Conservation Trust, and the Victorian new church, consecrated in 1877.

Elsecar Heritage Centre was formerly an ironworks and colliery workshops belonging to Earl Fitzwilliam of Wentworth Woodhouse (Walk 20, p86). The Darwin Company Ironworks were built first, and by 1800 two furnaces were producing pig iron for ranges, railways and the building trade.

The steam railway, opened in 1850, was primarily a mineral line. The tracks were lifted in 1984, but re-laid after Barnsley council bought the site in 1988 and began restoration.

Elsecar New Colliery, sunk in 1795, required a water pump. The Newcomen Beam Engine, the only one in the world still at its original location, ran until 1923, when electric pumps replaced it. To see the Beam Engine, cross the railway and immediately turn left along the Trans Pennine Trail for 50m.

Elsecar Park. PHOTO: David Coefield

27 Wombwell Ings & Gypsy Marsh

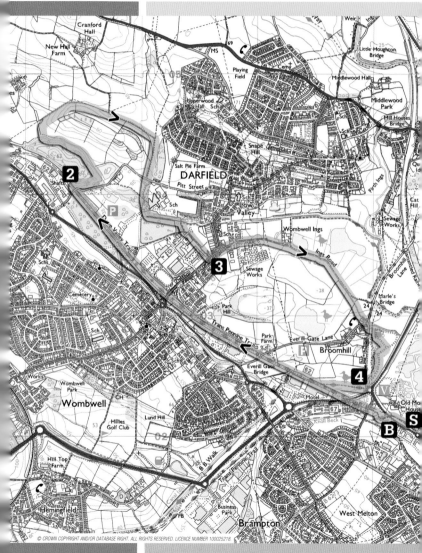

© CROWN COPYRIGHT AND/OR DATABASE RIGHT. ALL RIGHTS RESERVED. LICENCE NUMBER 100025218.

11.25 km / 7 miles

We start from Old Moor RSPB Reserve and head west along the Trans Pennine Trail to explore the River Dove and Netherwood Country Park using permissive paths. On the return we pass through two contrasting nature reserves managed by the RSPB. It can be combined into a figure-of-eight with Walk 23 (p106). Again, binoculars would greatly enhance your enjoyment of this walk.

START RSPB Old Moor on the A633.
GRID REF SE 423022.
PARKING RSPB Old Moor.
PUBLIC TRANSPORT
Bus services 222 and X20 (not Sundays). *Train* ffrom Sheffield, Meadowhall and Rotherham.

TERRAIN A mixture of surfaces. Much of this walk can be muddy at times.
REFRESHMENTS Café at the Visitor Centre. The Old Moor Tavern, Broomhill, *T* 01226 755455.
OS MAP Explorer 278, Sheffield, Barnsley and Rotherham, North sheet.

27 Wombwell Ings & Gypsy Marsh

S From the car park, cross the footbridge over Knoll Beck and turn **right** along the Trans Pennine Trail. Pass Elsecar Greenway and Gypsy Marsh and continue along the Trans Pennine Trail. You pass the lake of the former Park Hill Brickworks, Wombwell Recreation Ground, a racetrack and cross two more roads before reaching Bradberry Baulk Lane.

2 Cross over to the Silkstone Common railway sleeper post and turn **right** signed to Netherwood Country Park. Ignore the main path climbing left and continue parallel with the road. Turn **left** when you meet the Dove and follow the river to a footbridge. Cross this and head away from the river to a gate. Follow the permissive path **left** around the field boundaries to reach the exit gate. Turn **right** alongside the hedge towards Darfield and **right** again at the T-junction. Stick to the tarmac path, cross the road and continue along the improved path passing the school on your left. Cross the road bridge and immediately turn **left** across the grass to continue beside the river. Turn **right** at a wooden footbridge so the metal fence is on your left and continue beside the dyke to Station Road.

3 Cross over, turn **left** and continue straight ahead at the bend into Ings Road. At the Caravan Park, pass through the bridle gate into Wombwell Ings Nature Reserve (ings is a Norse word for wetlands). Bear **right** along the embankment, leave it at the hide and follow Bulling Dyke through the recreation area. Turn **right** along the road and enter Broomhill Park just past Old Moor Tavern (food). Turn **left** then **right**. Go **left** past the seats then **right**. Branch **left** at the playground and continue to a car park.

4   Turn **left**, cross the road and enter Gypsy Marsh Nature Reserve, a small pocket of surviving lowland heath, ablaze with orchids in late June and July. Turn **left** upon reaching the Trans Pennine Trail and return to Old Moor.

Netherwood Country Park.

28 Yorkshire Sculpture Park

© CROWN COPYRIGHT AND/OR DATABASE RIGHT. ALL RIGHTS RESERVED. LICENCE NUMBER 100025218.

Bretton Hall Country Park, set in 500 acres of 18th century parkland just off junction 38 of the M1, is home to the Yorkshire Sculpture Park. This route also takes in two of West Yorkshire's waymarked long distance trails, the Kirklees and Dearne Ways, to explore the countryside to the west of the Park.

START Bretton Hall Country Park.
GRID REF SE 295125.
PARKING There is free parking in a layby on the A637 Huddersfield Road, close to junction 38 of the M1 (grid ref: SE 296121). The main car park, which is 250m further on, is expensive but the money helps fund the Sculpture Park. *To enhance your enjoyment of the walk, I suggest obtaining a Sculpture Park leaflet from the box beside the toilets before setting out.*
PUBLIC TRANSPORT
Bus service Hourly service 96. Reduced service on Sundays.
Train from Sheffield and Rotherham.

TERRAIN An undulating walk on mostly natural paths. Stout footwear recommended.
REFRESHMENTS In Yorkshire Sculpture Park café and Exhibition Centre, *T* 01924 832631.
OS MAP Explorer 278, Sheffield, Barnsley and Rotherham, North sheet. Small section on Explorer 288.

28 Yorkshire Sculpture Park

S Park as far up the layby as possible past Jebb Lane. Just beyond, the pavement bears left to the old road, along which parking is forbidden. At the far end rejoin the pavement and in 100m turn **left** in front of a bungalow along the exit road leading out of the pay and display car park. Pass through the gate and carry on along the track to a seat, where bear **left** on the Lower Park and Lakeside path. *From the car park, take the gate to the left of the kiosk and toilets to reach the same point.* Follow the grassy path, which is reinforced with plastic mesh and turn **left** over the ornate Dam Head Bridge.

You pass three drystone wall enclosures, bearing Andy Goldsworthy's exhibit, Hanging Trees. Views open up on both sides as you approach the highest point. The Basket # 7 installation has moved to pastures new, but there are good views of Bretton Hall and the Emley Moor transmitter mast. Amongst the trees is a circular drystone enclosure, called Outclosure, also by Andy Goldsworthy.

2 Cross the head of the lake and bear **right**. Hidden away and rusting inside the quarry on your left is a sculpture by Serge Spitzer. Continue along the track and bear **left** into Oxley Bank Wood up the charred and oiled 71 steps, the work of David Nash. Note how a patchwork of tree roots has been exposed by erosion to form what could be described as footpath sculpture. Cross the squeezer stile in the corner and bear **left**, following the sandstone ridge of Oxley Bank.

Join the surfaced track and look to your right towards Bretton Hall. Sculptures are visible in the parkland to the right.

The Longside Gallery, situated inside a former indoor riding school, is shared by Yorkshire SP and the Hayward Gallery. It is free and open from 11am – 4pm, but check the website for dates and exhibitions.

3 Beyond the gallery, turn **right** and follow the walking route to Yorkshire Sculpture Park. This pleasant grassy trod has conveniently spaced benches. Note but do not cross the stile on the right just beyond the fourth. No path is discernible, so turn **left** and double back slightly to a stile in the fence. Keep **right** of the clump of trees and aim for the end tree on the horizon, where there is a stile. Descend the edge of the field to a road and turn **left** for 50m to a wall stile. Descend to a

Yorkshire Sculpture Park with Anthony Caro's Promenade 1996. PHOTO: YSP/Jonty Wilde

28 Yorkshire Sculpture Park

footbridge and continue alongside the hedge past Clayton Hall Farm and the house beyond.

4   OPTIONAL ROUTE

If you don't mind tarmac and short cuts, you may follow the lane going **right**.

Purists, on the other hand, should pass through the gap at the waymark post and join the Kirklees Way. Follow the hedge to a stile in the corner and continue on the waymarked route down the centre of the field, crossing two more stiles in quick succession. Descend the edge of the field and having crossed the stream turn **right** on a narrow path leading to a metal kissing gate beyond the electricity pole. Keep in this direction over two more fields and turn **right** along the track.

Bear **left** at the fork to a T-junction (**Optional Route** joins from the right) and turn **left**. Halfway between the river and road, a few yards beyond the second telephone pole, cross the stile on your right and head for the far left-hand corner. Turn **right** and walk along the bank of the infant Dearne. Head away from the river as you approach the bridge to a stile in the wall. Cross the road to the footpath opposite, go **straight on** and turn **right** at the gate. Bear **left** to the metal handrails and cross the footbridge over Bentley Brook. Bear **left** and ascend to a stile. Cross the field and join the hedge on your left. At the far end turn **left** along the bridleway to West Bretton, but after a few yards pass through the wooden gate on the right into Bretton Hall Country Park.

The 48km (30-mile) Dearne Way follows the river from its source on Birds Edge to its confluence with the River Don at Mexborough. The Kirklees Way is an 116km (72 mile) circular walk around the Kirklees district.

5 You may have your own agenda for exploring the Sculpture Park, but as a guide I suggest you bear **left** and follow the path up past the totem pole and through the sponsorship trellis. Pass the café and go **left** of the information point to the picnic area. Continue parallel with the road and cross over to the sinister-looking white-faced men, inspired by Aboriginal art and the ancient Greek warrior statues found in Riace in Italy in 1972. Pass Jonathan Borofsky's Molecule Man and head for the steps leading to the main exhibition area. Turn **left** through the hedge to visit the Bothy and Garden galleries before continuing round to the Visitor Centre and Underground Gallery, the major indoor exhibition site. Exhibits change annually.

If there is no access to the Formal Garden, continue back to the road, turn **left** and **left** again a little further down to join the dog walkers' route over the ha-ha bridge and into the woodland picnic site. Turn **right** and enter the open space known as *Henry Moore in the Park*. Bear **right** past the road-end to the fenced-in Deer Shelter.

Leave the Skyspace and head to the junction, where follow the track **left** to a stone enclosure. Bear **right** back towards the bridge and car park.

Henry Moore was born in Castleford in 1898. The park contains a significant number of his works. The Skyspace was created by James Turrell inside an eighteenth century grade II listed building, formerly a deer shelter. The underground chamber is lined with seats with a square aperture cut into the roof. Here you can sit in quiet contemplation for a few minutes looking up at the sky, the passing clouds and perhaps the falling rain.

PHOTO: John Coefield

29 Worsbrough Mill & Wentworth Castle

Wentworth Castle.

Starting from the 17th century working corn mill in Worsbrough Country Park, we pass through the Woodland Trust's infant Birdwell Wood to visit the remains of Rockley blast furnace and engine house. We then circuit the Parkland Trail through Stainborough Deer Park and visit the monuments of Wentworth Castle to complete an exceptional walk through beautiful countryside.

12 km / 7.5 miles

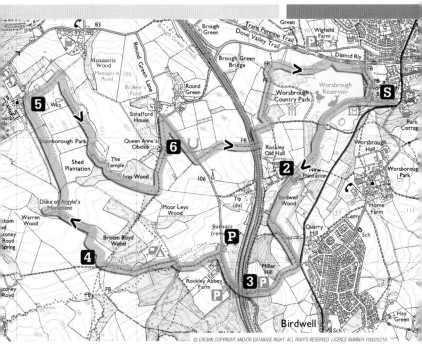

© CROWN COPYRIGHT AND/OR DATABASE RIGHT. ALL RIGHTS RESERVED. LICENCE NUMBER 100025218.

START Worsbrough Country Park on the A61 at Worsbrough Bridge, opposite the Red Lion.

GRID REF SE 351033.

PARKING Pay and Display car park at Worsbrough Mill.

PUBLIC TRANSPORT *Bus services* 66 or 265. Service 265 from Sheffield.

Train from Sheffield, Meadowhall and Rotherham, then the 66 or 265.

TERRAIN Mainly natural, but good grassy paths.

REFRESHMENTS Red Lion, Worsbrough Bridge, *T* 01226 280574. Café in Wentworth Castle Gardens.

OS MAP Explorer 278, Sheffield, Barnsley and Rotherham, North sheet.

29 Worsbrough Mill & Wentworth Castle

Worsbrough Mill is open weekends and all week during the school holidays 10am – 4pm. It is a working 17th century corn mill, lovingly restored and opened as an industrial museum in 1976. Originally water-driven, a steam engine was installed in 1843 to cope with an increasing demand for stone-ground flour. The engine had to be scrapped in 1922, from when the mill was used to crush ingredients for animal feed until its closure in the 1960s. During restoration, a 1911 Hornsby hot bulb oil engine was installed. Displays tell of the mill's history, and products are on sale in the shop. Entrance is free.

S Follow the lane from the car park and pass to the **left** of the museum through an information area. Cross the footbridge and turn **left** along the path hugging the southern shore of Worsbrough reservoir, built in 1796 as a header for the Dearne and Dove canal. The reservoir path joins a parallel bridleway and passes through an A-frame. Cross over a track and stile and continue beside Rockley Dike.

2 Ignore the footbridge crossing the stream at the end of the meadow and bear **left** to a stile with a short length of boardwalk beyond. Turn immediately **right** into the infant Birdwell Wood, planted by the Woodland Trust in the mid 1990s. Pass beneath overhead wires in a clearing and enter mature woodland. Turn **left** as you reach the M1 and ascend. Turn **left** at the top of the steep slope and continue in the same direction along the grassy path towards the road. Turn **right** just before reaching the exit and descend straight on at a junction to pass a redundant stile. Follow the waymark **right** downhill to a former car park.

The castellated Rockley Engine House was built in 1813 to pump water from iron workings in the area. Its Newcomen engine was removed to Chapeltown in 1870. Rockley blast furnace was built at the turn of the 18th century to smelt locally-mined iron ore using charcoal.

3 Pass under the motorway and continue along the road to a layby on the **right** just past Greensprings Touring Park. Ignore the signpost and enter the wood via the gap to visit Rockley Engine House. Take the path to the rear, turn **left** and cross the footbridge to the blast furnace. On the way back, bear **right** and follow the stream back to the layby.

Return to the caravan park entrance and follow the concrete drive through the kissing gate. You will be unlucky not to see a heron on the pond. Beyond the second pond the road crosses a bridge and enters the touring park. *Note the old, dilapidated stone bridge just upstream*. Walk all the way through and out the other side, where the road becomes an ascending farm track.

4 Enter Stainborough Park at the gate and follow the Parkland Trail. This seems to make a beeline for the Duke of Argyll monument, but turn **right** at a blue waymark into Broom Royd Wood. Follow the permissive path **left** to reach a gate and signpost. Divert **left** to visit the monument and return.

Pass through the gate, signed *Visitor Centre*, and continue straight ahead through the next gate. Either continue between the seats or follow the adjacent South Avenue, lined with oak and lime trees. Wentworth Castle soon comes into view. Bear **right** on the Parkland Trail through a gate in the deer fence, pass below the house and turn **left** at the waymarker to visit Wentworth Castle Gardens and Home Farm visitor centre, which houses a café, shop, toilets and information.

The Duke of Argyll monument (photo p137) was built in 1742 by William Wentworth. The statue on top is Minerva, the Roman name for the Greek Goddess, Athena. The column itself is modelled on one found in the basilica of Santa Maria Maggiore in Rome, which has an angel on top. Wentworth dedicated the monument to his father-in-law, the Duke of Argyll, in 1744.

The house and its estate were built by Sir Thomas Wentworth following a family feud. He expected to inherit Wentworth Woodhouse (Walk 20, p86) from the Earl of Strafford, but instead it went to a cousin. Thomas and his son William built and developed this site throughout the 1700s. The house has been home to the Northern College for Adult Education since 1978. The part of the gardens visible from here, called The Wilderness, look splendid in June when the rhododendrons are in bloom. There is a charge for a tour of the grade I listed gardens, which includes the Gothic folly of Stainborough Castle. Open 10am – 5pm. Brought to public attention through the BBC2 series Restoration in 2003, the estate is undergoing a massive programme of restoration, aided mainly by heritage lottery funding.

29 Worsbrough Mill & Wentworth Castle

The restored Palladian Bridge bears the date 1758. It spans the artificial Serpentine, begun in 1749 and extended to include the Temple Ponds in 1773. Most of the ponds have either dried up or become overgrown, but are expected to be restored in due course.

Queen Anne was a patron of Thomas Wentworth, conferring many of his titles. Thomas erected the obelisk in her honour in 1734, twenty years after her death.

5 Return to the Parkland Trail and take the signed **left** fork down to the Serpentine lakes.

Turn **right** in front of the bridge along the Parkland Trail, which winds pleasantly alongside the Serpentine. The resident herd of spotted fallow deer are usually to be seen along this stretch. Stay outside the wood until the rotunda comes into view and head up to the monument at the waymarker post. It was started in 1739, the year Thomas died, and completed by his son William in 1746. It is based on the temple of Hercules Saxanus at Tivoli in Italy.

Leave the deer park through the gate in the left-hand corner; turn **right** alongside the fence then **left** into Ivas Wood. Fork **right** at the next waymarker and leave the wood at a wooden gate. Cross the stile and continue alongside the wall for 100m before branching **right** at a signpost to a stile. Beyond a kissing gate is a cottage with Queen Anne's Obelisk behind.

6 The drive is private so please continue along the field path to the road and turn **right**. Turn **left** beyond an equestrian centre down Old Hall Road and **left** again immediately after crossing the M1. Follow the field boundary round to the **right** and turn **left** at the waymarked junction. The path bends **right** and re-enters Worsbrough Country Park through a kissing gate. Turn **left** and then **right** at the fork beyond the footbridge. Pass through an area of wet woodland and along the northern shore of the reservoir. Either cross the dam wall or go on a few metres and turn **right** and **right** again over the bridge back to the mill and car park.

Duke of Argyll monument.

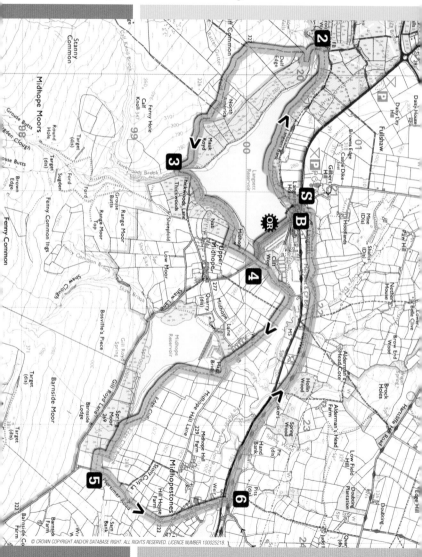

© CROWN COPYRIGHT AND/OR DATABASE RIGHT. ALL RIGHTS RESERVED. LICENCE NUMBER 100025218.

This walk explores the upper Don Valley, where a chain of three reservoirs were built in the late 19th century to provide drinking water for the growing populations of Sheffield and Barnsley. Starting from Langsett Barn, managed by the Peak National Park, we circuit the upper reservoir through woodland and over wild moorland before heading downstream past the middle reservoir to Midhopestones. The return is along a dismantled railway. A shorter loop of 5.5km circling the reservoir is included.

START The listed 15th century Langsett Barn on the A616.
GRID REF SE 210005.
PARKING Langsett Barn.
PUBLIC TRANSPORT
Train from Sheffield, Rotherham and Barnsley to Penistone then the two hourly 23 bus to Langsett (23a on Sundays). *Though not a long journey by public transport, the reliance on trains and an infrequent bus service makes timing critical.*

TERRAIN A fairly energetic walk with some moderate climbs. The moorland paths are good but stout footwear is recommended. The final stretch over pastureland can be rutted and wet.
REFRESHMENTS Bank View café, open every day 9am – 5pm, *T* 01226 762337. Waggon & Horses, Langsett, *T* 01226 763147; and Ye Olde Mustard Pot, Midhopestones, after 9km, *T* 01226 761155. Both pubs serve real ale and food.
OS MAP Explorer OL1, The Peak District, Dark Peak area, East sheet.

30 The Upper Don Valley

Work began on the dam in 1889 and took fifteen years. In those days, the only way of producing reasonable drinking water was to depopulate the catchment area of people and livestock. Six farms were lost in this way. The surrounding coniferous woods were planted in the 1920s to stabilize the steep banks. The extensive root systems effectively prevent soil erosion and provide a commercial return, with the majority of the wood pulped for paper. The reservoir and forest are owned and managed by Yorkshire Water.

The farm was destroyed by tank shells during practice for the Normandy landings in 1944. In order to accommodate the heavy armour, the track was strengthened with rubble from Sheffield houses destroyed in the Blitz – a sad chapter of local history beneath your feet.

S Leave the car park by the information panel in the left-hand corner and bear **right**.

The path eventually rises and leaves the plantation. Bear **right** at a fork to an open grassy space, where you will find a poetic seat. I mean literally – go look. From the seat you look down on Brookhouse Bridge, completed in 1904, which spans the Little Don, also called the River Porter. Both names allude to the colour of the peat-stained water, dun and port. I kid you not!

2 Descend to cross the river, pass through the gate on the **left** and ascend around the edge of the plantation to reach open moorland. The view improves with every step as you ascend Hingcliff Common to a junction by a waymarker post. Turn **left** and follow the path to North America, one of the depopulated farms. Pass through the ruins and the gate beyond.

3 Cross Thickwoods Brook, pass through a metal gate and continue alongside the low wall close to the waters' edge. Stay with the shoreline until you reach a waymark post, where you branch **right** up through the plantation. Turn **right** alongside a broken wall, continue past a way-marker post to a gate and turn **left** down Joseph Lane.

OPTIONAL ROUTE

You can shorten the walk here to 5.5km by turning **left** and following the road over the dam wall back to Langsett Barn.

4 Cross two fields to a stone stile and descend to a track. Turn **right** then immediately **left** back onto the footpath. Cross a stile and continue alongside the wall. Pass through two metal gates and eventually into an enclosed track with views along the valley. Bear **left** at the road and follow this quiet lane past the earthen dam of Midhope Reservoir. Turn **right** up steps at a footpath sign, ascend alongside the wall and enter the wood as the reservoir comes into view. Reaching a blocked-off gateway, descend and turn **left** alongside Edge Cliff Brook. Continue to the end of the wall; turn **right** for 100m, then **left**.

5 Turn **left** along Mortimer Road into Midhopestones (pronounced *Middup*) and turn **left** on a field path opposite Oaks Lane. A short distance to the left along the road is the church of St James the Less, noted for its boxed pews. Open to visitors, it is packed with photos and information and well worth a visit. Return along the road and turn **left** at Ye Olde Mustard Pot, built in 1760 as a farmhouse before becoming an alehouse called The Barrel in 1780. It was extended, refurbished and renamed in 2001. Pass Potters Well and cross the Little Don to reach the A616.

6 Cross the A616 and pass under the bridge. Follow the track **left** for 50m, then switch to the dismantled railway.
   For a while the line becomes a farm track before reverting to an embankment running through a more open landscape. Pass through two metal gates and branch **right** alongside the fence at the waymark post after 100m. Cross two wooden footbridges, one after the other, and continue parallel with the road through three waymarked metal kissing dates. 50m beyond the smaller gate, turn **left** over the wall stile and head for the building with measles, which is, in fact, the popular Bank View Café. Turn **right**, cross into the road opposite by the Waggon & Horses and follow it to the right to arrive at Langsett Barn by the toilets.

The Water Treatment Plant opened in 1985 to replace sand filter beds here and at Midhope. The works produce 60,000 cubic metres of water a day to serve a population of 200,000 in southwest Barnsley and northwest Sheffield.

William Gough established a pottery here in 1720. The well, which was the village's water supply until the 1930s, consists of two troughs – one supplied drinking water, the other the pottery. The well is decorated in early September along with the church in accordance with the ancient Derbyshire custom of well dressing.

The single track line was a branch of the Stocksbridge Railway, which opened in 1877 to serve the steelworks. It terminated at the quarry in Langsett and was used mainly during construction of the dams. It is discernible now only as a pleasant wooded footpath, part of the Barnsley Boundary Walk, whose waymarkers you follow back to Langsett.

Appendix

www.travelsouthyorkshire.com
Bus, train and tram timetable
information for the whole region.

www.barnsley.gov.uk
Click on *Barnsley museums* for
information and opening times
for Cannon Hall Museum, Elsecar
Heritage Centre, Worsbrough Mill
and Yorkshire Sculpture Park.

www.sheffield.gov.uk
Click on *Leisure and tourism*
for information on places visited
on the Sheffield walks.

www.heritagewoodsonline.co.uk
An informative website on
Fuelling a Revolution.

cistercians.shef.ac.uk/roche
History of Roche Abbey.

www.wentworthwoodhouse.co.uk
For details of tours and dates.

www.elsecar-heritage.com
Details of special events like steam days.

www.english-heritage.org.uk
Type in *Roche Abbey* or *Monk Bretton
Priory* for information and opening times.

www.monkbrettonpriory.org.uk
Detailed history of Monk Bretton Priory.

www.rspb.org.uk
Click *search* and enter *Old Moor* for
information, opening times and prices.

www.wentworthcastle.org
Information on Wentworth Castle
and its gardens.

Get in touch
E roberthaslam0@gmail.com
Tell me your favourite walks,
viewpoints and report any changes.

Any problems you encounter like
damage, obstructions or excessive litter
should be reported to the following:

Sheffield City Council: Parks &
Countryside on *T* 0114 250 0500
E parksandcountryside@sheffield.
gov.org

**Rotherham Metropolitan Borough
Council:** Streetpride on *T* 01709 336003.
E streetpride@rotherham.gov.uk

**Barnsley Metropolitan Borough
Council:** *T* 01226 770770
E online@barnsley.gov.uk

Notes